Easy Sewing

THE KWIK·SEW® WAY

by Kerstin Martensson

THE KWIK•SEW® WAY

Copyright © MMII **KWIK•SEW**® *Pattern Co., Inc.*

3000 Washington Avenue North
Minneapolis, MN 55411-1699 U.S.A.
www.kwiksew.com

Printed in the United States of America.

ISBN 0-913212-19-9

1 2 3 4 5 6 7 8 9

CONTENTS

INTRODUCTION

This book is for anyone who wants to learn to sew or get back to sewing. It explains how to get started and introduces you to up-to-date sewing techniques and ideas, that will make sewing quicker, easier, and fun. The experienced sewers will enjoy the simplicity of the patterns, and keep up with the changing methods and time saving techniques.

Sewing gives you an opportunity to be creative and develop a hobby which will last a lifetime. Once you learn to sew, you will never forget it.

With the introduction of fantastic new fabrics and the use of quick labor saving techniques adapted from the ready-to-wear manufacturers, you can really make it in one evening and wear it the next day.

In addition to being enjoyable, sewing will save you money, whether you sew for yourself or the entire family. Sewing can be as simple or as complicated as you wish it to be. Realizing how busy people are, we have tried to keep it as simple as possible.

A Master Pattern is included with this book to enable you to get started as soon as possible. Patterns for T-shirt, blouse, pants and skirts with many variations are included; you will be able to make a whole wardrobe.

The book has a chapter for each garment, followed by easy style changes. The last chapter includes creative ideas for embellishments, appliqués, trims, color blocking and much more.

Below all the photos throughout the book there will be an explanation of the garment, the style changes made, and the type of fabric used. The sewing procedures are easy to follow with many clear illustrations, that even a beginner sewer can follow and be able to make professional looking garments.

Enjoy yourself, have fun, and start sewing!

Basic blouse, lengthened 5" (12 cm). Side hemline slits.
Long straight skirt with hemline slit.
T-shirt. Fabric edging.
Fabric: Silk noil, T-shirt - Printed interlock

SEWING MACHINES

A sewing machine in good working order is the most important tool. It can be a very basic straight stitch and zigzag machine or a very elaborate electronic or computerized machine. Read your sewing machine manual carefully, and practice selecting the different stitches and functions. You can then easily switch from one stitch to another and avoid many frustrations. Whatever machine you use, it is important to keep it clean, and if necessary oiled.

Check the needle before sewing, to be sure it is not bent or blunt, as this could ruin your project. A bent or dull needle will have a tendency to make the machine skip stitches or pull the fabric down into the hole in the needle plate. We recommend keeping a supply of needles in various sizes.

A fine needle is used for lightweight fabrics and a larger needle is used for heavier fabrics. Needles are usually marked as follows: 11/75 for lightweight fabrics, 12/80 for medium weight fabrics and 14/90 for heavyweight fabrics. Use a ballpoint or a stretch needle for knits.

Any machine that sews a zigzag stitch can also do double needle stitching. Double needle stitching can be used for topstitching or hemming. A hem stitched with a double needle works well on knit fabrics because it has give. Purchase a few double needles with different spacing between the two needles.

A serger (overlock) machine is a wonderful tool to help speed up your sewing. This machine trims the edge of fabric, sews the seam, and overcasts in one step. When you use a serger (overlock) machine, be very careful to use the correct seam allowance as the knife trims the fabric, and the garment will not fit properly if you do not use the correct seam allowance.

There are many serger (overlock) machines on the market that can perform additional functions. We suggest reading the manual to become familiar with your particular brand of machine.

Certain functions cannot be done on a serger (overlock) machine, such as topstitching, buttonholes, patch pockets, zippers, etc., you need a regular sewing machine for those functions.

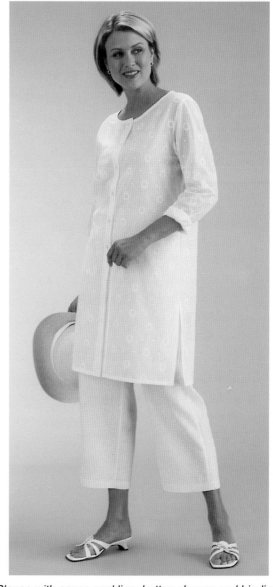

Blouse with scoop neckline, button closure and binding.
Tunic length. Side hemline slits.
Cropped pants.
Fabric: Linen

MASTER PATTERN

The Master Pattern includes T-shirts, blouses, pants, skirts and many variations and design changes. All the styles are simple, so you can get started right away with an easy and quick sewing project. With these basic patterns, you can make a complete wardrobe. After you have made all the basic garments, refer to KWIK & EASY DESIGN CHANGES for fun variations you can make on each garment.

The Master Pattern includes sizes Extra Small, Small, Medium, Large and Extra Large. Each size is printed in a different color to make it easy to follow when tracing. The Master Patterns are printed on both sides of the paper and you have to trace the pattern pieces. To trace the pattern, use tracing paper, or use a tracing cloth which is made from pressed fibers. The cloth is durable, will not tear and is transparent for easy tracing. Trace the pattern pieces for the size you have selected, and be sure to follow the same size on all the pattern pieces.

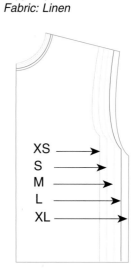

To make it easier for you to select the correct pattern pieces, each one is numbered and identified.

MASTER PATTERN PIECES

1. T-shirt Front
2. T-shirt Back
3. T-shirt Sleeve
4. T-shirt Crew Neckband
5. T-shirt Mock Turtle Neckband
6. T-shirt Neckline Binding
7. T-shirt V-neckband
8. T-shirt Front Neckline Facing
9. T-shirt Back Neckline Facing
10. T-shirt Hood
11. Blouse Front
12. Blouse Back
13. Blouse Sleeve
14. Blouse Upper Collar
15. Blouse Under Collar
16. Blouse Cuff
17. Blouse Slit Facing
18. Blouse Back Facing
19. Pockets
20. Pants Front
21. Pants Back
22. Pants Side Pocket Method I
23. Pants Side Pocket Method II
24. Straight Skirt
25. Gored Skirt

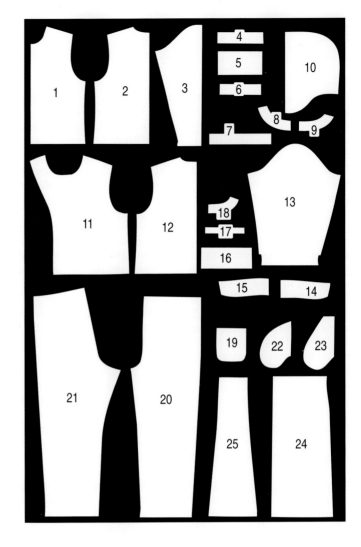

CHOOSING SIZE

The patterns are made to fit specific body measurements with ease allowed for comfort and style. Before you trace the pattern, it is necessary to determine which size to use.

Have a friend measure you to get the correct measurements. Be sure to wear proper under garments and shoes when being measured. Use a flexible tape measure made from fiberglass or vinyl.

Compare your measurements to the chart below and choose the size that is closest to your measurements. The measurements of the finished garment, at the fullest part of hip and/or bust, are given on the Master Pattern. By deducting the body measurement from the measurement of the finished garment, you will know the amount of ease the pattern has. This will help you to determine if you should use a smaller or a larger size if your measurements are between sizes.

BODY MEASUREMENTS

Size	XS	S	M	L	XL	
Bust	31½-32½ (80-83)	34-35½ (86-90)	37-38½ (94-98)	40-41½ (102-106)	43-45 (110-114)	" (cm)
Waist	22-23½ (56-60)	24¾-26 (63-66)	27½-29 (70-74)	31-33 (79-84)	35-37 (89-94)	" (cm)
Hip	32¼-34 (82-86)	35½-37 (90-94)	38½-40 (98-102)	41¾-43¾ (106-110)	45-47 (115-120)	" (cm)
Back Waist Length	15½ (39.5)	16 (41)	16½ (42)	17 (43)	17 (43)	" (cm)

BUST

The bust measurement is taken by placing the tape measure over the back, underneath the arms and over the largest point of the bust.

WAIST

Tie a piece of string or elastic around your waist to determine the position of the waist. Measure around the waist at the string position.

HIP

The hip measurement is taken over the widest portion of the hips.

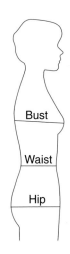

LENGTH OF SKIRT

Measure from the waist to the length you wish the skirt to be. Place the tape measure with the beginning of the numbers where you want the bottom of skirt. This way, it will be easy to read the measurement at the waist.

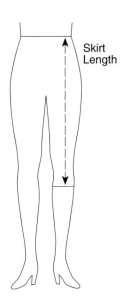

BACK WAIST LENGTH

Measure from the top of your backbone to your natural waistline. This measurement is important when making a garment with a fitted waist or a seam in the waist area. If your back waist length measurement is different than the chart, shorten or lengthen the garment above the waist.

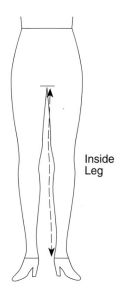

LENGTH OF PANTS

For the length of pants, you need to measure the inside leg seam and the crotch depth. To measure the inside leg seam, measure from the crotch to the length you wish the pants to be.

LENGTH OF SHIRT OR BLOUSE

Measure your back from the top of the backbone to the length you wish the finished garment to be.

SHOULDER AND ARM LENGTH

Tie a string loosely around the neck to determine the neckline. Bend your arm slightly, measure from the string to the bone at the tip of the shoulder and continue measuring over your elbow to your wrist bone.

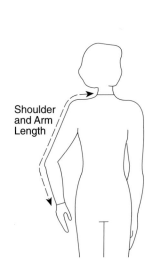

CROTCH DEPTH

To obtain your crotch measurement, sit on a flat table or a hard chair that does not have any curves in the seat. At the side, measure from the waist over the hip to the top of the table or chair.

Refer to Page 58 for crotch depth adjustments

ADJUSTING LENGTH

Before cutting out the garment, be sure to compare the finished length given in each section with the length you wish the garment to be. The Master Pattern pieces have shorten and lengthen lines marked.

To lengthen the pattern, cut the pattern apart on the shorten and lengthen line. Place a strip of paper underneath the pattern and tape in place. Extend the grain of fabric line to the added paper. Measure from the shorten and lengthen line the amount you wish to lengthen the pattern and draw a parallel line on the paper. Place the other part of the pattern along the drawn line, be sure to match the grain of fabric line and tape in place. Connect the lines on the sides and trim the excess paper.

To shorten the pattern, measure from the shorten and lengthen line the amount you wish to shorten the pattern and draw a parallel line. Cut the pattern apart on the shorten and lengthen line and place the edge on the drawn line, overlapping the pieces. Tape in place and connect the lines on the sides. Be sure to make the same adjustments on the front and the back pattern pieces.

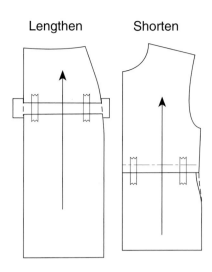

Lengthen   Shorten

Long gored skirt. Pullover top with neckline binding.
Fabric: Polyester crepe

Basic blouse. Side hemline slits. Contrast insets.
Long straight skirt with hemline slits. Contrast insets.
Fabric: Satin backed rayon suiting

FABRICS

There are basically two kinds of fabrics, knit and woven, made from either natural or synthetic fibers or a blend of both. Combining synthetic and natural fibers gives an almost unlimited variety. In selecting fabric for your sewing project, examine the fabric to see how it feels, drapes, does it wrinkle easily, or ravel.

It is important to choose a fabric that will compliment the pattern design, look attractive on the person wearing the garment, and perform according to your expectations. To determine if the fabric is suitable for the pattern, be sure to check the suggested fabrics. It is important to know if the pattern is designed for a knit or woven fabric, and if it is for light, medium, heavy, soft or crisp fabric.

It is also a good idea to drape a yard or two of the fabric on yourself, gather it at the waist and look in a mirror. You can see if the color and texture are complimentary, and if the fabric falls close to the body or stands away from the body. If the fabric stands away from the body, choose styles that are straight. If the fabric is soft, you can choose styles with more fullness or gathers.

When purchasing the fabric, take note if the pattern pieces should be cut in one direction. If the fabric is cut this way, it sometimes requires more fabric. All fabrics with nap, such as velvet, corduroy, velour and terry should be cut in one direction. Fabrics with a one-way design and all knits should also be cut in one direction.

Allow extra fabric for shrinkage, usually all fabrics with cotton will shrink to some degree. Allow extra fabric for matching stripes, plaids and large designs.

PRE-WASHING FABRIC

Any fabric that is washable should be pre-washed before you cut out the garment. Use the same detergent and the same setting on your washer and dryer as you will for the finished garment. Pre-washing will eliminate the possibility of the garment shrinking the first time it is washed. It is very discouraging to do all the work of making a garment only to find that is has shrunk after the first wash. Do not pre-wash ribbings as it will make it difficult to sew.

STRETCH KNITS

When you are using patterns designed for stretch knits, it is important to use fabric with the degree of stretch the pattern recommends. Use the stretch charts given on Page 10.

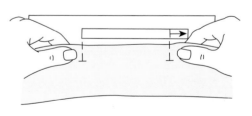

To test the fabric for the degree of stretch, fold the crosswise edge of the fabric approximately 3" (8 cm). Mark 4" (10 cm) with pins. Hold the 4" (10 cm) of the folded fabric against the chart and stretch gently to the outside line. If the fabric stretches easily, without excessive rolling, to this line or slightly farther, the fabric has the correct amount of stretch for the pattern.

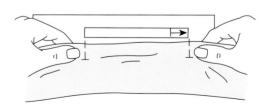

If you use a fabric that has more stretch than recommended, your garment will have a looser fit. If the fabric stretches less, it will have a closer fit. You should not use a woven fabric when the pattern is designed for a knit fabric, or a knit fabric when a woven fabric is recommended. Some patterns are designed for both woven and knit fabrics, in that case, use stable knits which have a very small degree of stretch. It is also a good time to check the knit fabric for recovery, if the fabric does not return to its original shape after stretching, it could sag and stretch out of shape when the garment is worn.

STRETCH CHARTS

Fabric with 25% stretch across the grain such as: Interlock, Jersey, Thermal Knit, Velour

| 4" (10 cm) of Knit Fabric should stretch | to at least | here. |

Fabric with 35% stretch across the grain such as: Sweater Fabric, Velour, Stretch Terry, Interlock

| 4" (10 cm) of Knit Fabric should stretch | to at least here. |

Fabric with 75% stretch across the grain such as: Swimwear Fabric, Fabric with Spandex or Lycra®

| 4" (10 cm) of Knit Fabric should stretch | to at least here. |

Fabric with 100% stretch across the grain such as: Ribbing

| 4" (10 cm) of Knit Fabric should stretch | to at least here. |

INTERFACING

Interfacing is used to support and shape details, such as collars, cuffs, pockets, waistbands, and button and snap closures. Interfacings are available in fusible or sew-in types in a variety of weights. They are available in white, off-white, gray and black. It is much easier to use fusible interfacing, it can be used on almost any fabric, except some delicate and textured fabrics. Choose interfacing according to the weight of the fabric and the shaping needed. Always test your interfacing on a scrap of the garment fabric to see if the result is satisfactory.

Fusible knit interfacing works well on lightweight knit or woven fabrics. If you wish to have a little more body, we recommend, using a woven fusible interfacing from a blend of polyester and rayon. It still feels soft, but gives more body. For applying fusible interfacing, follow the manufacturer's directions.

The easiest way to use fusible interfacing for small pattern pieces is to fuse the interfacing to the fabric before you cut out the pieces. Place the glue side of the interfacing to the wrong side of the fabric, use a steam iron and fuse the interfacing to the fabric; make sure to use an up and down motion to eliminate the possibility of stretching the fabric out of shape. Then fold the fabric piece and cut out the pattern piece.

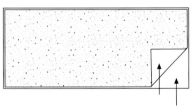
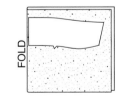

GLUE SIDE OF INTERFACING
TO WRONG SIDE OF FABRIC

Basic Blouse, lengthened 7" (18 cm). Hemmed sleeve.
Fabric: Crinkled polyester sheer

Sew-in interfacing is basted to the wrong side of the cut out pattern piece. When basting the interfacing, be sure to sew both sides in the same direction to keep the interfacing from shifting. On a collar, baste each side from the center back.

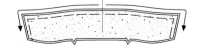

THREAD

Use an all purpose thread, available in cotton, cotton wrapped with polyester, or 100% polyester thread. Always use the same thread for the bobbin and the needle on the sewing machine.

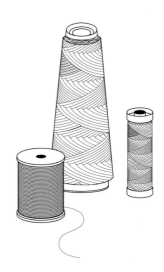

If you are unable to find a color thread exactly the same as the color of the fabric, choose a slightly lighter shade, as it will usually blend better than a darker shade.

Thread for the serger (overlock) machines are available in large and small tubes and cones. Choose a good quality lightweight thread to make the seams less bulky. The serger thread does not necessarily have to match the garment, you can combine different colors to make them blend with the fabric.

ELASTIC

Elastics are available in a variety of widths and finishes. They can be knitted, woven or braided. Knitted and woven elastics retain their original width when stretched, curl less, and can be stitched directly to the garment. Braided and non-roll elastics are best used in casings. We recommend pre-washing all elastics, to avoid shrinkage after the garment is made.

CUTTING

A pair of sharp scissors is necessary for cutting any type of fabric. If your scissors are dull, get them sharpened as soon as possible. Sewing scissors should not be used for cutting paper or other household tasks, they will dull quickly.

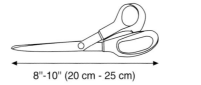

8"-10" (20 cm - 25 cm)

For cutting fabric, we recommend a pair of scissors 8" - 10" (20 cm - 25 cm). You will also need a smaller pair for cutting threads and trimming.

It is best to cover the table with a cutting mat to protect your table, and to prevent the fabric from slipping. The mats are available in most fabric stores.

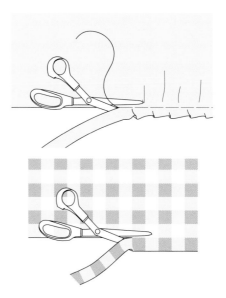

A rotary cutter is a very helpful tool, it has to be used with a special plastic cutting mat that protects the cutting surface and the blade. The mats are available in different sizes, you will have more use for a larger mat; it can be stored under a bed, or some can be rolled up for storage.

If the fabric is wrinkled, press the fabric. If the fabric has a sharp crease at the fold, try to press out the crease, or avoid placing it where it will readily show on the garment.

Fabrics have two finished edges, along the lengthwise edges, called selvages. To make the cut ends straight on woven fabric, clip the selvage and pull one of the crosswise threads from selvage to selvage. Cut along this line to obtain a straight edge. If the fabric has visible lines, cut along one line.

It is sometimes difficult to tell the right and the wrong side of the fabric. If you can not tell, choose the side you prefer and be sure to use the same side throughout the garment.

If making a garment from striped fabric, be sure to fold the fabric, matching the stripes. To match the stripes on a shirt, place the bottom of the front and the back pattern pieces on the same stripe. If using sleeves, place the underarms of the sleeves on the same stripe as the underarm of the front and back.

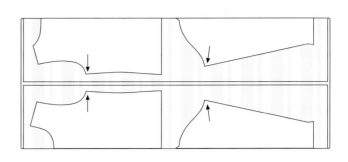

Accurate cutting and marking of the garment is very important. If the garment is cut exactly as the pattern and the markings are made carefully, it will be much easier to sew.

Place the pattern pieces on the fabric, following the grain of fabric line and the stretch of fabric line in the correct direction. Place all the pattern pieces on the fabric before you start cutting. Save scraps of fabric to test stitching, pressing and trial buttonholes.

Layouts show the placements of the pattern pieces on the fabric. Some layouts show the fabric folded double lengthwise, right sides together, with the selvages together, other layouts show the fabric folded with the selvages in the middle. When folding the fabric, be sure that the fold is along the grain, measure from the selvage to the fold along the length of the fabric to be sure the fold is an even distance from the selvage. When using knit fabric, make sure that the fold of the fabric is along a lengthwise rib.

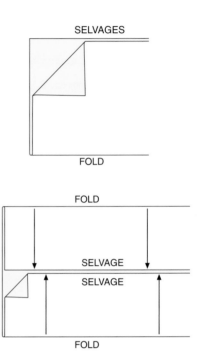

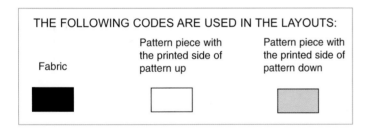

THE FOLLOWING CODES ARE USED IN THE LAYOUTS:

Fabric

Pattern piece with the printed side of pattern up

Pattern piece with the printed side of pattern down

If the layouts show both sides of a pattern piece, and half is shaded, follow these procedures: Cut out all the other pattern pieces first, allowing fabric for the shaded area. Fold the remaining fabric along the grain and place the pattern piece on the fabric along the fold and cut out the pattern piece.

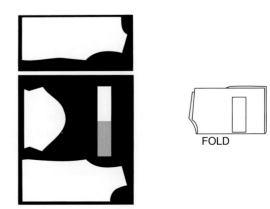

Sometimes the pattern pieces are too wide to be placed on the folded fabric. In this case, fold the fabric crosswise, right sides together, and cut the fabric apart along the fold from selvage to selvage. Turn one layer of the fabric and place, right sides together, so the arrows on both layers are in the same direction.

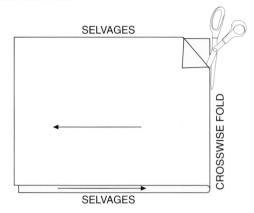

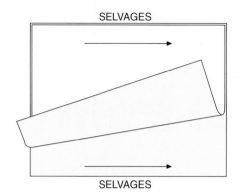

If the layout shows a pattern piece extending from the layout, cut all the other pattern pieces first, then unfold the fabric and cut the pattern piece on single layer of fabric.

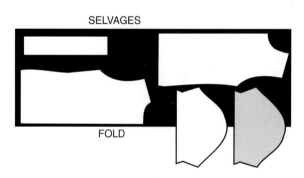

When the pattern pieces are cut on a single layer of fabric, the fabric is usually placed right side up. Be sure to follow the layouts to determine if the pattern is placed with the printed side of pattern up or down. If you are cutting a left and a right side of a garment, you have to cut one with the printed side of pattern up and one with the printed side of pattern down.

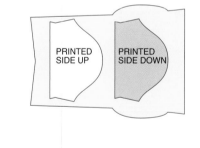

For securing the pattern pieces to the fabric, use fine pins with colored heads. Some sewers prefer to use weights instead of pins to hold the pattern pieces in place. You can buy special weights for this purpose or you can use silverware, cans, cups, etc., as long as they keep the pattern steady on the fabric. Large metal washers, available in hardware or plumbing supply stores, make excellent weights. They are smooth and relatively inexpensive. If they are not heavy enough, you can tape several together.

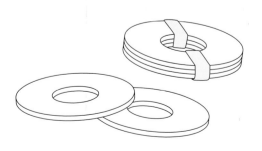

MARKING

After cutting, it is a good idea to label each piece on the wrong side, so you do not mix them up. We recommend using transparent tape with a dull finish that you can write on. Place small pieces of the tape on the wrong side of the fabric, marking front, back, side seams, etc., always use a pencil, as a ball point pen could spot the fabric and ink is difficult to remove.

Be careful when you are using transparent tape on velour, stretch terry, or other fabrics with a similar surface, as it may mark the fabric. Try the tape on a piece of scrap fabric before you use it on your sewing project.

Rather than cutting around the notches and to mark the center front, center back and the fold lines, make tiny clips on the seam allowances, clip only 1/8" (3 mm), these clips are more accurate and much faster to make. On some fabrics such as sweater knits or loosely woven fabrics, use a water soluble pen for marking.

Markings for the position of pockets, buttonholes, etc. have to be transferred from the paper pattern piece to the right side of the fabric. This can be done, using pins, water soluble pen, or chalk.

To mark, insert a pin through the pattern and the fabric. Lift the pattern piece and one layer of the fabric and insert a pin to each layer of the fabric at the pin or make a small mark with a water soluble pen.

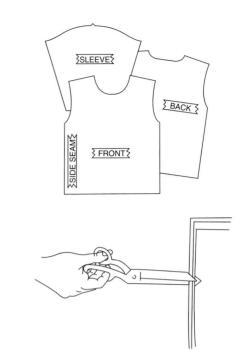

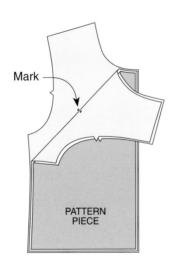

Mark

PATTERN PIECE

PATTERN PIECE

THE FOLLOWING FABRIC ILLUSTRATION CODES ARE USED IN THE SEWING INSTRUCTIONS:

Right Side of Fabric

Wrong Side of Fabric

Interfacing

Basic blouse. Breast pocket.
Fabric: Cotton shirting

14

SEAMS AND SEAM FINISHES

When sewing the seams, the type of stitch to use will depend on the fabric, the type of sewing machine and the width of the seam allowance.

Before you start to sew the garment, take a small piece of the scrap fabric that your garment is cut from, double the fabric and sew a row of straight stitches. Check the stitches to be sure the thread tensions are correct. You have a perfect thread tension when the top and the bottom tensions are exactly equal and the knot cannot be seen. Adjust the tensions so that the stitches appear the same on both sides, see illustration. Try to adjust only the top tension, as this is easier to do on all sewing machines. In some cases, you may need to adjust both the top and the bottom tensions.

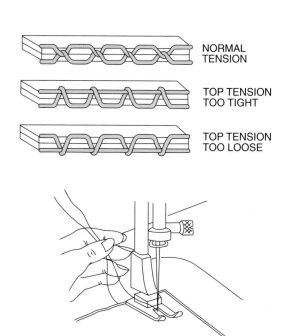

NORMAL TENSION

TOP TENSION TOO TIGHT

TOP TENSION TOO LOOSE

TO MAKE A SEAM

Pin two pieces of fabric, right sides and raw edges together, unless otherwise specified in the instructions. You will find it much easier to start a seam if you lower the needle into the fabric and hold both the top and bobbin threads behind the presser foot. As the machine starts to sew, slowly pull these threads to help the machine feed the fabric and to eliminate the tendency of the fabric to bunch up under the presser foot. Sew the seam. To secure the stitches at the beginning and at the end of the seam, backstitch a few stitches on seam line.

SEAMS FOR KNIT FABRIC
USING 1/4" (6 mm) SEAM ALLOWANCE

REVERSE CYCLE MACHINE
Sew the seam, using an overlock stitch. This stitch sews and overcasts in one step. It is not necessary to stretch the fabric while sewing, as this is an elastic seam.

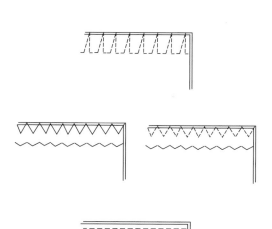

ZIGZAG MACHINE
Sew the seam, using a narrow zigzag width and a medium stitch length. This seam will stretch with the fabric. Overcast the seam allowances together with a large zigzag stitch or a three-step zigzag stitch.

STRAIGHT STITCH MACHINE
Sew the seam, using a medium stitch length and stretch the fabric in the front and in the back of the presser foot as you sew. Sew another seam on the seam allowance close to the raw edges to keep seam allowances together.

SERGER (OVERLOCK) MACHINE
This type of sewing machine gives a professional look. Serger (overlock) machines sew, overcast and trim the excess seam allowances in one step. When using a serger (overlock) machine, be sure to use the correct seam allowance so the garment will fit properly.

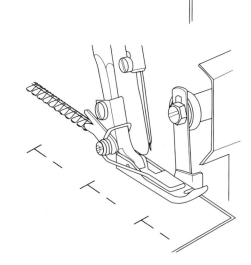

Serger (overlock) machines will not sew over pins. Pin only when necessary and remove the pins well ahead of the knife, or pin far over to the left of the cut edges. Remove the pins after the seam is completed.

SEAMS FOR WOVEN FABRIC
USING 1/4" (6 mm) SEAM ALLOWANCE

Sew the seams with a medium length straight stitch. Overcast the raw edges together, using a medium zigzag stitch, three-step zigzag stitch, or use the serger (overlock) machine.

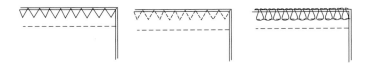

SEAMS FOR FIRM KNIT AND WOVEN FABRIC
USING 5/8" (1.5 cm) SEAM ALLOWANCE

Sew the seams, using a medium length straight stitch. If the fabric requires overcasting, overcast the edges before sewing the seam, using a zigzag stitch, a three-step zigzag stitch, a straight stitch close to the raw edges, or use a serger (overlock) machine.

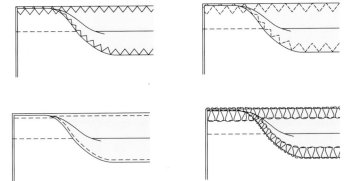

STITCH LENGTH

Instructions refer to the stitch length as short, medium and long. The number of stitches per inch or centimeter determines the stitch length.

Short	12-20 stitches per inch, 6-8 stitches per centimeter
Medium	10-12 stitches per inch 4-5 stitches per centimeter
Long	5-8 stitches per inch 2-3 stitches per centimeter
Satin stitching	35-50 stitches per inch 15-20 stitches per centimeter

SEAM RIPPING

If you have a seam that you have to change, gently pull the fabric apart, and using a seam ripper, cut the threads in between the fabrics.

Another way to remove the seam is to cut the stitches on one side at about 1" (2.5 cm) intervals, then pull the thread on the other side.

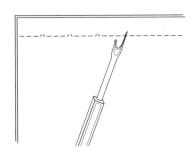

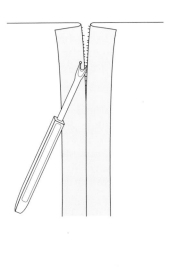

SEWING TERMS

The following sewing terms are used in this book and in pattern instruction sheets. The step-by-step instructions will tell you the sewing term, but not the procedures.

GRADING

Grade seams by trimming the seam allowances to graduated widths. When sewing with 5/8" (1.5 cm) seam allowances, one seam allowance is trimmed to 3/8" (1 cm) and the other to a scant 1/4" (6 mm). Remember that the seam allowance that will be next to the outside of the garment should be the wider one. For example, if you are grading a collar, the upper collar seam allowance should be the wider one.

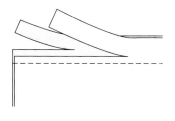

UNDERSTITCHING

Understitching is sewing the seam allowances to one side, such as on a facing, it prevents the seam from rolling to the outside of the garment and it also makes it easier to press. Before understitching, clip any curved seam allowances. Fold the seam allowances toward the facing as you are sewing on the right side of facing close to the seam. Trim the seam allowances close to the stitches to reduce bulk, if necessary.

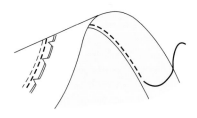

STITCHING IN THE DITCH

Stitching in the ditch is straight stitching, on the right side of the garment, close to or in the well of the seam. It is used to secure collars, facings and bindings. The stitches will not be readily visible if done carefully.

Using a binding as an example, sew one edge of the binding to the garment and press the binding toward the seam allowances. Fold the binding to the wrong side over the seam allowances and pin. It is best to pin on the right side, so the pins can be easily removed when sewing. On the right side, sew as close as possible to the seam, using a zipper foot.

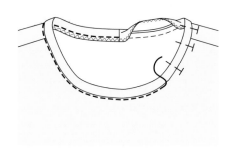

EASING AND GATHERING

One or two rows of straight stitching with a long stitch length and looser upper thread tension. Sew on the seam line and again in the middle of the seam allowance. To gather, pull the bobbin thread and secure by wrapping around a pin as shown.

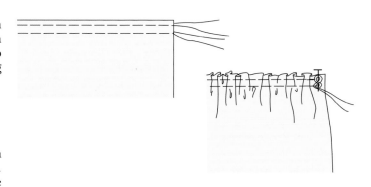

STAYSTITCHING

Staystitching is straight stitching on one layer of fabric on seam line of a curved area, such as on a pocket or a neckline. Staystitching prevents these areas from stretching while handling. It is also used at corners where clipping the seam allowances to the corners will be necessary, in this case, use a short stitch length.

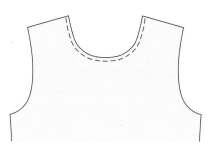
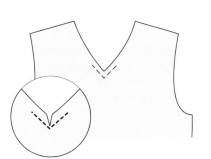

HEMS

The easiest way to hem a garment is to topstitch the hem. Overcast the raw edge, fold the hem to the wrong side and press. Pin the hem in place and sew close to the overcasted edge with a straight stitch.

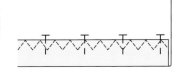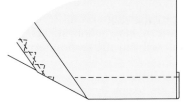

When hemming a knit fabric, sew with a narrow zigzag width and a medium stitch length. Or, an attractive finish can be obtained if you use a double needle. Refer to your sewing machine manual for using a double needle.

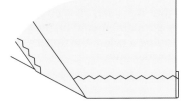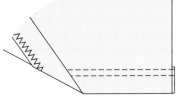

BLIND HEMS

If you prefer to have a blind hem, you can make the hem on the machine or by hand. Overcast the raw edge of the hem. Fold the hem to the wrong side and press. Pin the hem in place. See your sewing machine manual for blind hem instructions.

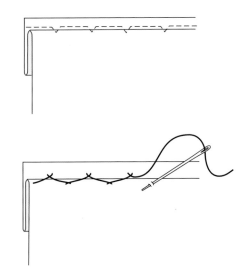

To hem by hand, turn the hem back and working from the left to the right, make a small horizontal stitch on the garment, make another stitch in the hem diagonally across from the first stitch. Make the stitches in a zigzag pattern.

NARROW HEMS

Narrow hems can be done single or double. Single hems work well on medium to heavyweight woven fabrics and on knits. Double hems are used on lightweight and sheer fabrics.

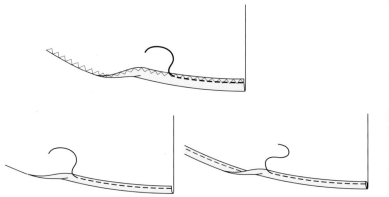

SINGLE HEM - Overcast the raw edge, fold 1/4" (6 mm) or 3/8" (1 cm) to the wrong side and press. Sew close to the edge of hem.

DOUBLE HEM - Fold 1/8" (3 mm) to the wrong side and sew close to the edge. Press the hem. Fold again along the raw edge and sew a second seam. Press the hem.

LETTUCE EDGING

Lettuce edging can be done on stretchy knit fabrics and it makes a pretty finish on a top at the bottom edge and at the sleeves.

Set the machine to a medium or slightly wider zigzag width and a short stitch length. Fold the bottom edge 1/8" (3 mm) to the wrong side and zigzag over the folded edge, stretching the edge as much as possible while stitching. Note: Try the lettuce edging on a scrap of the same fabric and adjust the width and the length of the stitches for the desired look.

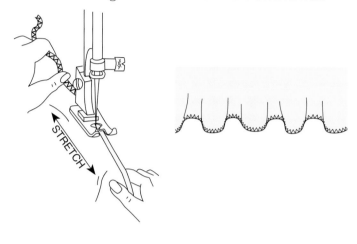

TOPSTITCHING

Topstitching can be decorative as well as functional. Decorative topstitching can add detail to a rather simple garment. For topstitching use a matching color thread, or if you can not find a perfect color, use a lighter color thread. Topstitching with a contrast color thread gives a sporty look, for example, on a navy garment use white thread. If you are topstitching with a contrast color, be sure your topstitching is perfect, otherwise it will take away from a well-made garment. Always make a sample on a piece of the same fabric and test the color and the stitch length.

Topstitching can also be done using a double needle. Double needles can be purchased with different spacing between the needles. Topstitching with a double needle works nicely on knits because the stitches have a certain degree of give.

All outside edges of a garment can be topstitched with one or two rows of topstitching. Topstitch on the right side of the garment close to the outside edge or 1/4" (6 mm) from the edge. If making two rows of topstitching, the first row should be close to the outside edge and the second row 1/4" (6 mm) from the edge or from the first topstitching.

When topstitching a collar and front edges of a blouse, start stitching on the inside of the right front at the bottom edge. At the corners of collar, topstitch as illustrated.

Basic T-shirt, shortened 2" (5 cm). Lettuce edging.
Fabric: Cotton interlock

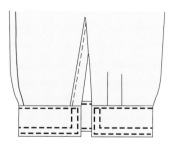

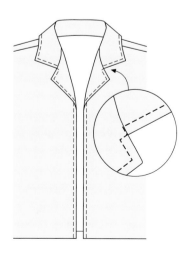

Hint: It can be difficult to topstitch an outside corner, to make it easy, insert a thread to the corner and after pivoting, pull on this thread to help the machine feed the fabric.

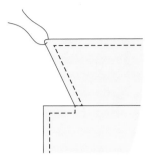

Topstitching can also be used to hold the seam allowances in place. After sewing the seam, press the seam allowances toward the side that will be topstitched, and topstitch through the garment and the seam allowances close to the seam. Topstitch shoulder seams on the back and armhole seams on the front and the back.

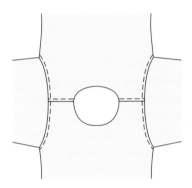

Basic blouse. Long sleeves with cuffs. Dress 26" (66 cm) length from waist. Breast pocket, button and buttonhole. Fabric: Polyester shantung

BIAS STRIPS

You may need a bias strip of fabric to finish a neckline, armholes, or to make ties and loops. Cutting the strips on the true bias is very important, if not cut on the true bias, they will twist. The true bias is the diagonal line between the crosswise and the lengthwise grain of fabric. To cut the strips, fold the fabric diagonally, placing the crosswise grain parallel to the lengthwise grain; the fold is the true bias. Press this fold gently and cut fabric apart along the fold to make the first bias cut.

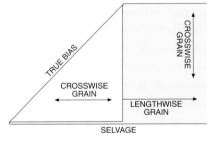
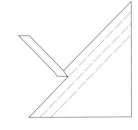

Measure and mark parallel lines, the width desired, with a chalk or a water soluble pen. Cut the strips.

If you need to join the bias pieces, place the **right side** of one piece to the **wrong side** of the other piece and cut the ends, following the straight grain as shown.

Pin ends, **right sides together**, matching seam lines and stitch. Press the seam open, and trim the extending seam allowances.

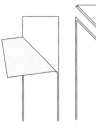

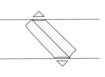

BUTTONHOLES AND BUTTONS

Before making buttonholes, check your sewing machine manual, as the procedure varies for different sewing machines.

Buttonholes can be horizontal or vertical and are placed on the right front. The size of the buttonhole should be 1/8" (2 mm) larger than the button. Always make a test buttonhole on a scrap of fabric to check the size and the stitches. If you are making vertical buttonholes, place the buttonholes along the center front. If you are making horizontal buttonholes, start the buttonhole 1/8" (2 mm) from the center front toward the front edge.

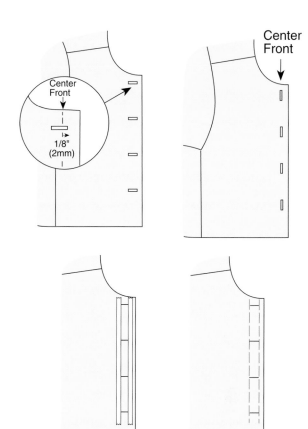

If you are using an electronic machine, where the buttonholes can be programmed so each one will be exactly the same length, you only have to mark the beginning of the buttonhole with a pin. If you are using a machine that does not have this function, it is a good idea to mark the start and the end of the buttonhole. An easy way, is to place pieces of tape at the beginning and at the end of the buttonhole and mark the buttonhole with a water soluble pen. On some fabrics, you should not use tape, in that case, mark the lines with basting stitches.

Cut the buttonhole open. It is a good idea to place pins at the ends of the buttonhole at cross angles to prevent cutting the ends and perhaps ruining your garment.

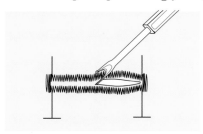

Sew the buttons to the left front along the center front to match the buttonholes. Buttons can be sewn either by machine or by hand. If you are using the machine, refer to your sewing machine manual.

There are two types of buttons, with or without a shank. Buttons with a shank have to be sewn by hand. Those without a shank can be sewn by hand or by machine.

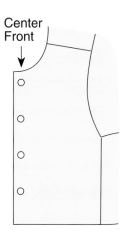

If buttons are for decorative use only, sew them directly to the garment. If buttons are used for a closure, allow enough space between the button and the garment to accommodate the fabric that the button will hold. The easiest way to do this is to place a toothpick or a large needle over the button between the holes. Sew the button and remove the toothpick or the needle. Wind the thread under the button a few times to make a shank. Secure the thread with a couple of stitches on the wrong side under the button.

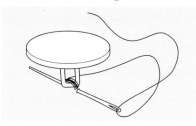

PRESSING

A good steam iron is necessary when you are sewing. Be sure to press each seam after it is sewn, and the finished garment will look professionally made. Make sure your iron is set at the temperature recommended for the fabric you are using. If you are not sure of the content of the fabric, always use a cooler setting to be on the safe side. A too hot iron used on polyester, will melt the fabric; used on wool, it could scorch the fabric.

The difference between ironing and pressing is, when ironing, you move the iron over the fabric with long back and forth strokes, using pressure and heat to remove the creases and the wrinkles in the fabric. Pressing is a press-lift, press-lift motion. When working with textured fabric and napped fabrics, the iron should not touch the fabric, the heat and the steam do the work.

After sewing the seams, press the seam allowances flat in the same direction as they were sewn. If the seam allowances are 1/4" (6 mm), press the seam allowances to one side, for the 5/8" (1.5 cm) seam allowances press them open, unless otherwise stated in the step-by-step instructions.

When pressing a blind hem, steam press the hem, and on the wrong side, press under the edge of hem to avoid a hem line showing on the right side of the garment.

It is best to do all the pressing on the wrong side of the garment. If pressing is needed on the right side, always use a press cloth.

A pressing ham is very helpful, especially when pressing necklines on sweaters and T-shirts. It is also useful when pressing darts, sleeve caps and areas that are curved.

PRESSING HAM

A point presser is used to press the seam allowances open on difficult to open areas, such as collars and cuffs. Collars will always look professionally made, if the seams are pressed open before turning.

A sleeve board is used for pressing sleeve seams.

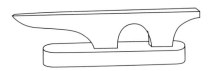

POINT PRESSER

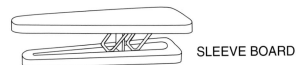

SLEEVE BOARD

Clip the curved seam allowances before pressing. On outside curves, cut out wedge shaped notches along the curve. On inside curves, clip the seam allowances to the stitches.

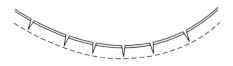

You can make a variety of T-shirts and Tops, using the Master Pattern. The shirt is slightly fitted and can be made with short or full length sleeves. Pattern includes six different necklines: Crew neckline, mock turtleneck, V-neckline, boat neckline, round neckline with self fabric binding, and a hood.

For the T-shirts and Tops, use stretch knits only with 25% stretch across the grain, such as interlock, jersey, textured knits, stretch velour, pointelle jersey, and thermal knits.

The mock turtle neckband and the crew neckband can be made from self fabric or ribbing. Use ribbings with 100% stretch, which are readily available in most fabric stores. Ribbings vary in degree of stretch. If using a ribbing with a different degree of stretch, the length of the neckband may need to be adjusted. If ribbing is soft and has more stretch, the neckband needs to be shortened, if ribbing is heavy and has less stretch, the neckband needs to be lengthened. Be sure to compare the stretch of the fabric and the ribbing with the stretch charts, on Page 10.

When sewing the knit tops, be sure to use the correct stitches. See Page 15 for seams on knit fabric, using 1/4" (6 mm) seam allowance.

The measurement of the finished garment is given on the front pattern piece. Check for the correct length of the shirt and the sleeves and adjust the pattern pieces, if necessary.

The finished length of the shirt at center back from the natural neckline is:

XS	S	M	L	XL
20 3/4"	21"	21 1/2"	22"	22 1/4"
52.5 cm	53.5 cm	55 cm	56 cm	56.5 cm

The finished length of the shoulder and full length sleeve from the natural neckline is:

XS	S	M	L	XL
27"	27 3/4"	28 1/2"	29 3/8"	30"
68 cm	70 cm	72 cm	74 cm	76 cm

To measure for the correct sleeve length, see Page 6.

Basic T-shirt.
Fabric: Cotton interlock

BASIC T-SHIRT

Use Master Pattern pieces:
1. Front
2. Back
3. Sleeve
4. Crew Neckband

Trace the pattern pieces, and on the front and the back, follow **neckline B**. Follow the line for the long or the short sleeve. Decide if you wish to make the neckband from ribbing or self fabric, and follow the correct line when tracing the neckband.

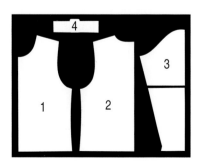

Compare the finished length of shirt and sleeve given above to the length you wish to have and make all the adjustments on the traced pattern pieces.

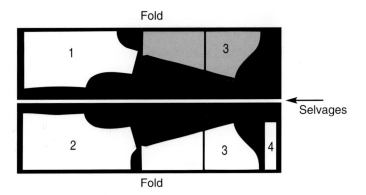

The fabric requirement is given on Page 86. If you have lengthened or shortened the pattern, take this into consideration when purchasing the fabric.

Place the pattern pieces on the fabric, following the layout. The pattern piece for the sleeve has to be used twice and placed on the fold. Be sure to follow the lines for the grain and the stretch-of-fabric. Cut out the shirt. Cut the neckband from ribbing or self fabric.

Note: Knits should be sewn with stretch stitches. For the correct stitches to use, refer to Page 15.

SHOULDER SEAMS

It is a good idea to stabilize the shoulder seams so they do not stretch out. Cut two pieces of the self fabric or fusible interfacing, on the lengthwise grain, the length of shoulder and 1/2" (1.3 cm) wide.

Pin or fuse the stabilizing strips to the wrong side of front shoulders. Pin the front to the back, right sides together, at the shoulder seams and sew through all three layers. Press the seam allowances toward the back.

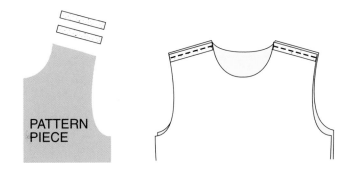

NECKLINE

Finish the neckline before you proceed with the rest of the shirt. Sew the ends of neckband, right sides together, using a straight stitch, and press the seam allowances open.

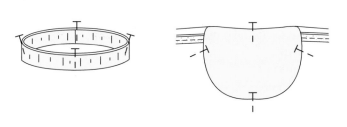

Fold the neckband in half lengthwise with wrong sides and raw edges together. Divide the neckband into fourths with pins. Divide the neckline into fourths with pins by placing pins at the center front, center back and equal distances between these two pins. NOTE: The pins will not be at the shoulder seams.

Pin the neckband to the right side of neckline with all the raw edges together, matching the seam on neckband to the pin at center back and the remaining pins.

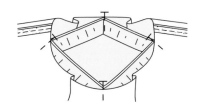

24

Sew the neckband to the neckline, stretching the neckband between the pins to fit the neckline. The easiest way to sew this is to have the smaller piece on the top. In this case, the neckline is underneath and the neckband on top.

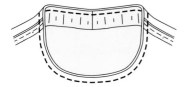 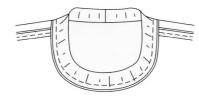 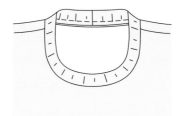

It is very important to press the neckline after it is sewn to obtain a professional look. Place the neckline over a pressing ham and steam press the neckline into shape, with the seam allowances toward the shirt. Be sure to press with an up and down motion.

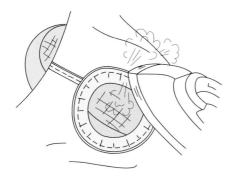

SLEEVES
The left and right sleeves are the same on this shirt. Pin the sleeves to the armholes, right sides together, matching the notches on sleeves to the shoulder seams, and the underarm edges. Sew the sleeves in place.

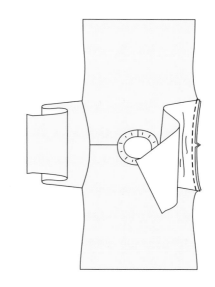

SIDE SEAMS
Pin the front to the back at the side seams and sleeve seams, right sides together, matching underarm seams. Sew the side seam and sleeve seam in one continuous step, starting at the bottom of the shirt.

Overcast the bottom edges of shirt and sleeves. Fold the 1" (2.5 cm) hems to the wrong side, press and pin. Stitch hems, see Page 18 for stitches.

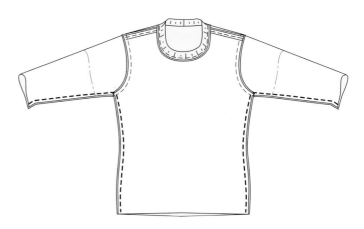

MOCK TURTLENECK

You can easily make a shirt with a mock turtleneck, using the same pattern pieces as for the Basic T-shirt on Page 23, except, **use pattern piece 5 for the neckband**. Trace the pattern pieces, and on the front and the back, follow **neckline A**. Decide if you wish to make the neckband from ribbing or self fabric. When tracing the pattern piece for the neckband, be sure to follow the line marked for ribbing or self fabric.

The construction is the same as for the Basic T-shirt, follow the instructions on Pages 24 and 25.

NECKLINE BINDING

The neckline of the shirt can be finished with a binding from the self fabric or a contrast color fabric with the same amount of stretch. The binding will show on the right side, and will be approximately 5/8" (1.5 cm) wide when finished. Use the same pattern pieces as for the Basic T-shirt on Page 23, except, use **pattern piece 6 for the binding**. Trace the pattern pieces, and on the front and the back, follow **neckline A**.

Sew the shoulder seams, following Page 24.

Sew the ends of binding, right sides together, using a straight stitch and press the seam allowances open.

Fold the binding in half, wrong sides and raw edges together, and press. Divide the binding and the neckline into fourths with pins.

 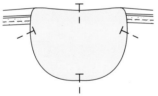

T-shirt. Neckline binding.
Appliqué using paper backed fusible web.
Fabric: Cotton interlock

Pin the binding to the **wrong side** of neckline with all raw edges together, matching the pins and the seam on binding to the center back. Sew the neckline 1/4" (6 mm) from edge, using a narrow zigzag stitch.

Understitch the neckline seam allowances to the front and back, using a narrow zigzag stitch. See Sewing Terms on Page 17. The understitching is done on the shirt side, because the binding will be folded and stitched to the outside of the shirt. Trim the seam allowances close to the stitches.

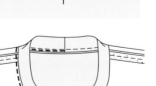 

Fold the binding on the seam line to the right side of shirt, press and pin. Topstitch close to the edge of binding, using a straight stitch or a double needle.

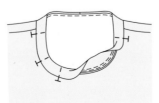 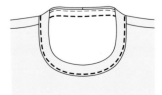

V-NECK

A V-neckline makes an attractive variation for a shirt and it is very easy to make. Use the same pattern pieces as for the Basic T-shirt on Page 23, except, use **pattern piece 7 for the neckband**. Trace the pattern pieces, and on the front and the back, follow **neckline C**. Cut out the shirt and cut the neckband from the self fabric or a contrast fabric with the same degree of stretch.

On the front, staystitch the point of V, using a short straight stitch, 1/4" (6 mm) from the raw edge and pivot at point of V. Clip the seam allowance to the stitches at the point of V.

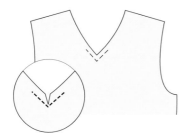

Sew the shoulder seams, following Page 24.

Fold the neckband, right sides together, and sew the center back seam, using a straight stitch. Press the seam allowances open. Fold the neckband in half, wrong sides and raw edges together, and press.

Pin the neckband to the right side of the neckline with the raw edges together, matching the center fronts, the seam on neckband to the center back, and the notches to the shoulder seams. Sew the neckband to the neckline with a straight stitch, stretching the neckband to fit the neckline. Start sewing at the center back, follow the staystitching on the front, and continue sewing the other side to the center back. Clip the seam allowances on the neckband to the point of V.

Press the neckline seam allowances toward the shirt. Fold the front and the neckband, right sides together, along the center front. Place a piece of tape on the neckband in line with the center front fold. Sew the center front seam of the neckband along the edge of the tape from the outer edge of neckband to the seam.

Overcast the neckline seam allowances together. Open the center front seam on the neckband and attach with a few stitches by hand.

Continue to sew the shirt as previously described.

T-shirt, lengthened 7" (18 cm). V-neck. Straight skirt. Fabric: Sweater knit

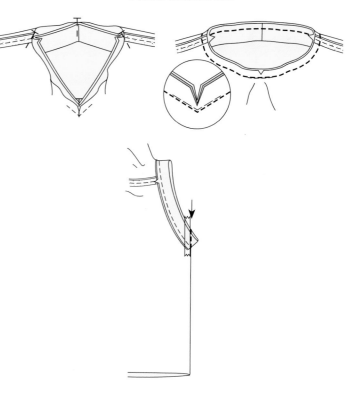

SHIRT WITH HOOD

A pullover shirt with a hood makes a sporty junior look. Use the same pattern pieces as for the Basic T-shirt on Page 23, except, use **pattern piece 10 for the hood** instead of the neckband. Trace the pattern pieces, and on the front and the back, follow **neckline B**. Cut out the shirt.

To prevent the neckline and the shoulders from stretching, stabilize the shoulders and the back neckline as follows: Use the back pattern piece and cut a piece of non-fusible interfacing 1" (2.5 cm) wide, following the neckline and shoulders. Be sure to place the center back on the fold when cutting the interfacing. Pin the interfacing to the wrong side of the back at shoulders and neckline and stitch 1/4" (6 mm) from edges.

Sew the front to the back at the shoulder seams, right sides together. Press the seam allowances toward the front.

Sew the hood pieces, right sides together, at the center back and top seam. Overcast the outer edge of the hood facing. Fold the hood facing on the fold line to the wrong side, and press.

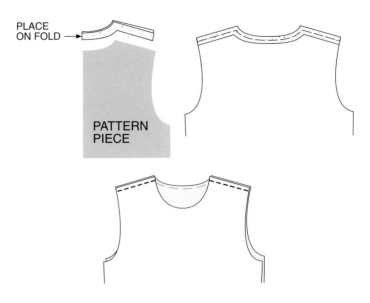

PLACE ON FOLD →

PATTERN PIECE

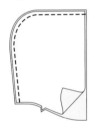

Pin the front edges of hood, right sides together, and mark 3/4" (2 cm) above the neckline. Sew from the neckline to the mark, along the fold line (crease), using a straight stitch. Fold the hood facing on the fold line to the wrong side, and sew close to the edge of facing.

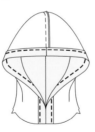

3/4" (2 cm)

Pin the hood to the neckline, right sides together, matching the center back seam to the center back, the notches to the shoulder seams, and the center front seam to the center front. Sew the hood to the neckline. Trim the interfacing close to the stitches. Continue to sew the shirt as previously described.

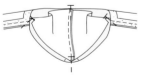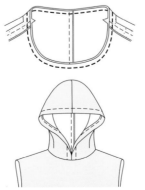

TRIM

Shirt with hood, lengthened 4" (10 cm). One size larger. Fabric: Textured fleece

SHIRT WITH HOOD AND ZIPPER

Use the same pattern pieces as for the Basic T-shirt on Page 23, except use **pattern piece 10 for the hood** instead of the neckband. Trace the pattern pieces, and on the front and the back, follow **neckline B**. On the front, add 1/4" (6 mm) to the center front edge. When cutting, be sure to cut two fronts.

To determine the length of zipper, measure the front edge and deduct the hem allowance and the neckline seam allowance. Purchase a separating zipper that length or longer, the zipper will be trimmed if too long.

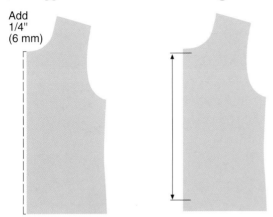

Pin the right side of zipper to the right side of front at the front edge, placing the zipper stop 1" (2.5 cm) above the bottom edge (hemline); if the zipper is too long, it will extend above the neckline. Using a zipper foot, stitch 3/8" (1 cm) from the edge of zipper tape. Sew the other side of zipper to the other front, using the same procedures.

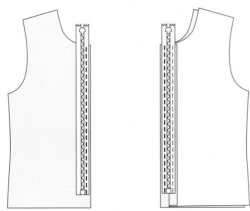

Fold the zipper to the wrong side and topstitch 1/4" (6 mm) from seams. Stabilize the back neckline and shoulders and sew the shoulder seams, as described for Shirt with Hood.

Sew the hood pieces, right sides together, at the center back and top seam. Overcast the edge of hood facing. Fold the hood facing on the fold line to the wrong side, and press.

Shirt with hood and zipper. Lower pockets.
Fabric: Cotton interlock

29

Pin the hood to the neckline, right sides together, matching the center back seam to the center back, the notches to the shoulder seams, and the fold lines on hood to the edges of fronts. Sew the hood to the neckline. Fold the hood facing on the fold lines to the wrong side over the zipper, and sew, following the previous stitches. Trim the excess length of zipper.

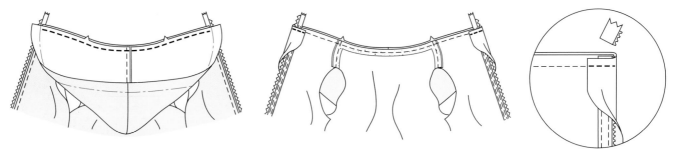

Turn the hood facing to the wrong side and pin. Sew close to edge of the hood facing.

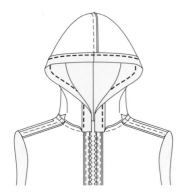

Continue to sew the shirt as previously described.

TOP WITH BOAT NECKLINE

The neckline of this top is finished with facings.
Use Master Pattern pieces:

1. Front
2. Back
3. Sleeve
8. Front Neckline Facing
9. Back Neckline Facing

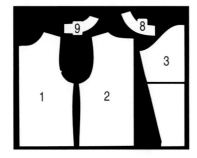

Trace the pattern pieces, and on the front and the back, follow **neckline D**. Compare the finished length of Top given on Page 23, and shorten or lengthen the pattern, if necessary.

Top with boat neckline.
Fabric: Printed stretch velvet

The fabric requirement is given on Page 86. If you have lengthened or shortened the pattern, take this into consideration before purchasing the fabric. Place the pattern pieces on the fabric, following the layout. Cut out the Top.

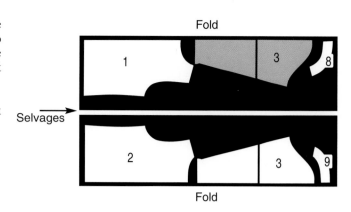

Cut lightweight fusible interfacing for the front and the back neckline facings, and fuse to the wrong side of facings.

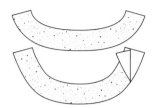

Sew the front facing to the back facing, right sides together, at the shoulder seams. Press the seam allowances toward the front facing. Overcast the outer edge of facing. Sew the front to the back, right sides together, at the shoulder seams. Press the seam allowances toward the back.

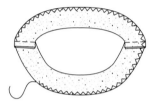

Pin the facing to the neckline, right sides together, matching the center back, center front, and the shoulder seams. Sew the neckline, and clip the seam allowances.

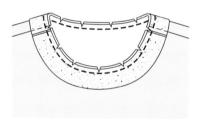

Understitch the seam allowances to the facing. This will prevent the seam from showing on the outside of the garment. See Sewing Terms on Page 17.

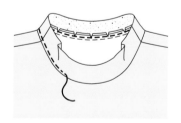

Fold the facing to the inside and press. Attach the facing to the shoulder seams.

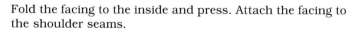

If desired, topstitch the neckline 1" (2.5 cm) from the neckline edge. Continue to sew the top as previously described.

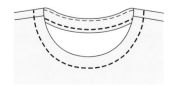

31

BOAT NECKLINE WITH SLIT

You can make a variation on the boat neckline by adding a slit at the center front.

Adjust the pattern piece for the front facing as follows: Extend the center front line 2" (5 cm). Make the facing 1" (2.5 cm) wide at the bottom edge and draw a curved line to the outer edge of the facing, as shown. Cut interfacing for the front and back facings and fuse to the wrong side of facings. On the interfaced side of the front facing, draw a 3" (8 cm) line along the center front for the slit.

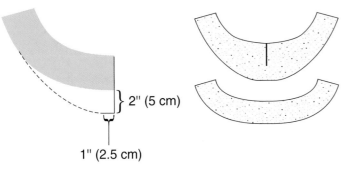

Sew the shoulder seams of the top and the facings as previously described.

Pin the facing to the neckline, right sides together, matching the center front, center back, and the shoulder seams. Sew the neckline and at the center front, sew 1/8" (3 mm) on each side of the line, pivoting at the end of line; use a short stitch length on the slit. Cut between the stitching lines from the neckline to the end of stitches. Trim the corners and clip the curved seam allowances.

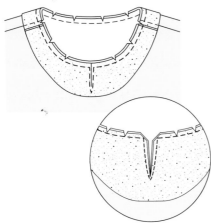

Understitch the neckline seam allowances to the facing, starting and stopping as close as possible to the slit edges, see Sewing Terms on Page 17. Turn the facing to the wrong side and press. Attach the facing to the shoulder seams.

Topstitch the neckline and the slit 1/4" (6 mm) from the edges. Continue to sew the top as described previously.

Top. Boat neckline with slit.
Fabric: Cotton interlock

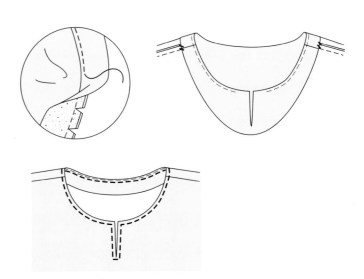

SHIRT WITH COWL COLLAR

For a shirt with a cowl collar, use the same pattern pieces as for the Basic T-Shirt, Page 23, eliminating the neckband. Trace the pattern pieces, and on the front and the back, follow **neckline D**.

For the collar, cut a piece of the self fabric 10" (25 cm) wide and the following length:

XS	S	M	L	XL
24"	24 1/2"	25"	25 1/2"	26"
61 cm	62 cm	64 cm	65 cm	66 cm

Be sure to cut the collar with the stretch of the fabric on the length of the piece.

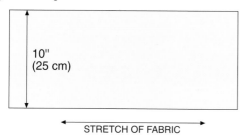

Pin the ends of collar right sides together. Mark 2 1/2" (6 cm) from one edge. Sew the collar to the mark, see illustration. Turn the collar right side out, finish sewing the remaining seam, **wrong sides together**, and press.

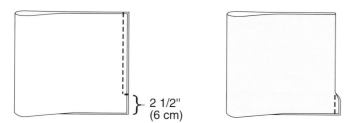

Overcast the edge with the seam on the wrong side. Divide the other edge into fourths and mark with pins.

Sew the shoulder seams as described previously. Divide the neckline into fourths with pins.

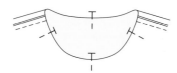

Pin the **wrong side of collar** to the **right side of neckline**, matching the seam on collar to the center back and the pins. Sew the collar to the neckline. Continue to sew the shirt as previously described.

Shirt with cowl collar.
Fabric: Polyester knit with metallic fibers

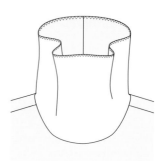

33

FABRIC EDGING

The neckline and bottom edges of sleeves of a knit top can be finished with fabric edging. Fabric edging is a strip of fabric which encases the garment edge. It can be an attractive trim, especially if using a contrast fabric or a fabric with a different texture. Be sure to use knit fabric with 25% stretch.

To determine the length of edging for the neckline, measure the front and the back pattern pieces at the outer edge of the neckline. Double this measurement and deduct 1/2" (1.3 cm). Cut the edging piece 1 3/4" (4.5 cm) wide, with the stretch of fabric on the length of the piece.

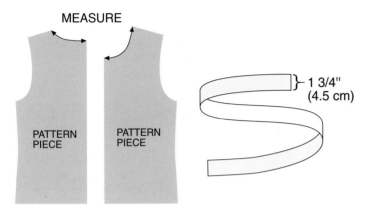

To determine the length of the edging for a sleeve, eliminate the hem on the bottom edge. Measure the bottom edge, double this measurement and deduct 3/4" (2 cm).

Sew the shoulder seams as previously described. Sew the ends of the edging, right sides together, and press the seam allowances open. Overcast one edge of the piece. Divide the edging and the neckline into fourths with pins.

Pin the edging to the neckline, right sides together, matching the seam to the center back and the pins. Sew the neckline **3/8" (1 cm)** from the edge. Fold the edging over the seam allowances to the wrong side and pin. From the right side, "Stitch in the ditch" to secure the edging on the inside, see Sewing Terms on Page 17.

T-shirt, neckline D. Fabric edging.
Dress 26" (66 cm) length from waist.
Short sleeves, shortened 4" (10 cm).
Fabric: Matte jersey

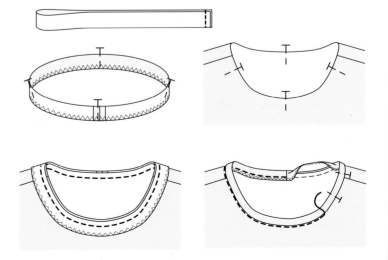

34

SHIRT WITH COLLAR AND ZIPPER

For this shirt with an exposed zipper, you can use a fancy rhinestone zipper, a sporty zipper with heavy plastic teeth or a regular zipper to make shirts with completely different looks.

Use the same pattern pieces as for the Basic T-shirt, except, **use pattern piece 5 for the collar**. Trace the pattern pieces, and on the front and the back, follow **neckline A**.

Use a 9" (22 cm) zipper. Cut a strip of fusible interfacing 1/2" (1.3 cm) wide and 7 1/2" (19 cm) long. On the side without the glue, draw a 7" (18 cm) long line in the center of the strip. On the wrong side of the front, mark the center front with basting stitches or a water soluble pen.

Place the interfacing piece on the wrong side of the front, matching the marked lines and fuse. Staystitch 1/8" (3 mm) on each side of the line marked, and across the bottom of the marked line. Cut between the stitching lines from the neckline to 1/4" (6 mm) above the bottom of the staystitches, and clip to the corners of stitches.

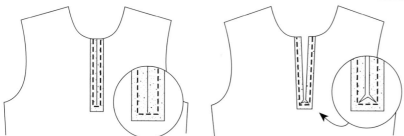

Shirt with collar and zipper.
Fabric: Printed jersey

Sew the shoulder seams as previously described. Fold the collar in half lengthwise, wrong sides and raw edges together, and press. Divide the collar and the neckline into fourths and mark with pins. Pin one edge of the collar to the neckline, right sides together, matching the pins. Sew the neckline and press the seam allowances toward the collar.

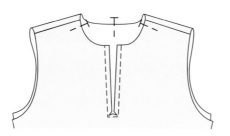

Place the right side of zipper to the right side of front with the zipper stop along the bottom staystitching. The zipper is in the opposite direction from the cut opening. Hold the zipper in place with transparent tape. Using a zipper foot, sew across the width of zipper teeth, following the staystitching, start and stop exactly at the corners. Remove the tape.

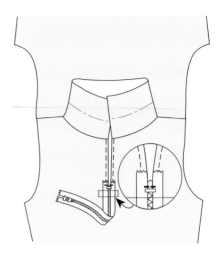

Fold the zipper toward the neckline. Pin the right side of front to the right side of zipper with zipper pull at the crease on collar. Place the staystitching close to the zipper teeth. Using a zipper foot, sew the front and collar to the zipper, following the staystitching. Repeat for the other side of zipper.

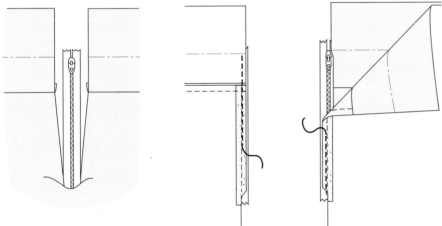

At the top of zipper, fold the extending zipper tape toward the center front and pin. Fold the extending collar on the crease to the right side over the zipper. Sew the ends of the collar, following the stitches for inserting zipper.

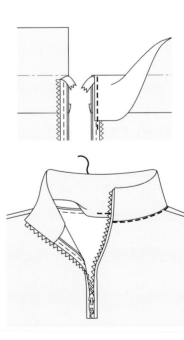

Turn the collar right side out. Pin the free edge of collar to the neckline over the seam. On the right side, "Stitch in the ditch" to secure the collar on the inside, see Sewing Terms on Page 17. Topstitch zipper 1/4" (6 mm) from the seams, as shown. Continue to sew the shirt as previously described.

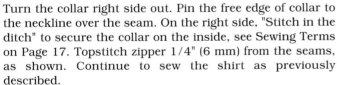

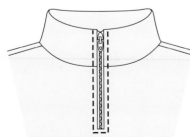

CARDIGAN

The neckline of the cardigan will be finished with a binding from the same fabric as the cardigan. It will have a loop and button or a hook and eye closure at the neckline.

Use the same pattern pieces as for the Basic T-shirt on Page 23, except **use pattern piece 6 for the binding** instead of the neckband.

Trace the pattern pieces, and on the front and the back, follow **neckline A**. On the front pattern piece, add 3/4" (2 cm) to the center front edge for facings. When cutting the cardigan, be sure to cut two fronts.

Add
3/4"
(2 cm)

*Cardigan.
Fabric: Sweater knit*

Cut interfacing pieces for the front facings 3/4" (2 cm) wide and the length of the front. Place the interfacing on the wrong side of the fronts as shown, and fuse. Overcast the outer edges of the front facings. Fold the facings to the wrong side and press. Sew the facings to the neckline close to the edges to keep in place.

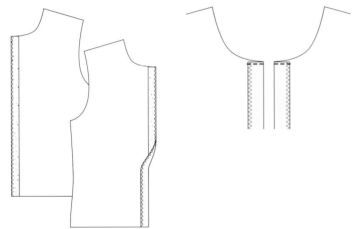

Sew the shoulder seams as previously described. Fold each end of the binding, right sides together, and stitch the ends. Trim the corners and turn right side out. Fold the binding in half, wrong sides and raw edges together, and press. Divide the binding and the neckline into fourths with pins.

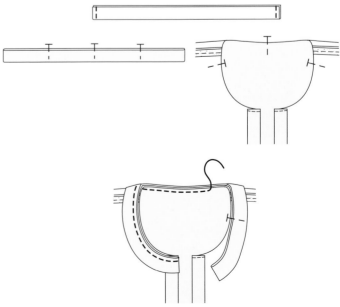

Pin the binding to the **wrong side** of neckline with all the raw edges together, matching the pins and the ends of the binding even with the front edges. Sew the neckline 1/4" (6 mm) from the raw edges, using a narrow zigzag stitch.

Understitch the neckline seam allowances to the front and back, using a narrow zigzag, see Sewing Terms on Page 17. Trim the neckline seam allowances close to the stitches. Fold the binding on the seam line to the right side, press and pin. Topstitch close to the edge of binding, using a straight stitch or a double needle.

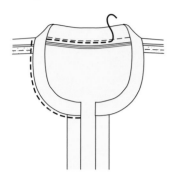 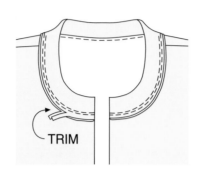 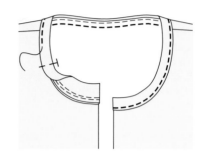

Sew the sleeves, the side seams, and the sleeve seams as previously described.

At the bottom edges of fronts, fold the facings on the creases to the right side and sew across the facings 1" (2.5 cm) above the bottom edge. Trim the hems on the facings. Turn the facings to the wrong side, and press.

Hem the bottom edge and the sleeves, refer to Page 18.

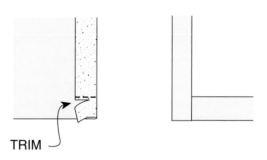

If desired, sew the facings to the fronts close to the edges of facings.

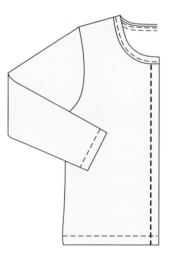

Sew a button to the end of the binding on the left front. Make a thread loop on the right front to match the button, or sew a hook and eye to the inside for closure.

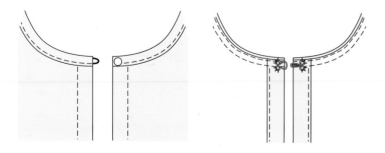

A variety of blouses can be made, using the Master Pattern, including full length sleeves with cuffs, hemmed full length or short sleeves, and with a collar or a scoop neckline with facings. By using different fabrics and changing the length, you can make completely different looks. You can also make several styles of pullover tops from the basic blouse pattern by making just a few easy changes on the pattern. For the blouse we recommend light to medium weight woven fabrics. Use cotton and linen types, such as broadcloth, chambray, sheeting, lightweight denim, rayon and rayon blends, such as challis. Silky fabrics can also be used, but are more difficult to sew. These include silk, silk like fabrics, charmeuse, crepe, and crepe de chine.

For your first blouse, use a lightweight cotton type fabric. Using a print fabric will hide "not so perfect" sewing.

The finished length of the blouse at the center back from the natural neckline is:

XS	S	M	L	XL
20 3/4"	21"	21 1/2"	22"	22 1/4"
52.5 cm	53.5 cm	55 cm	56 cm	56.5 cm

The finished length of the shoulder and the full length sleeve from neckline is:

XS	S	M	L	XL
28"	28 1/2"	29"	29 1/2"	30 1/2"
71 cm	72 cm	74 cm	75 cm	77 cm

To measure for the correct sleeve length, see Page 6.

Basic blouse. Long sleeves with cuffs.
Fabric: Rayon crepe

BASIC BLOUSE

The blouse has a collar, the fronts have fold back facings and button closure. It can be made with full length sleeves and cuffs, or with hemmed full length or short sleeves.

Use Master pattern pieces:

11. Front
12. Back
13. Sleeves
14. Upper Collar
15. Under Collar
16. Cuffs (if making long sleeves with cuffs)
17. Sleeve Slit Facing (if making long sleeves with cuffs)

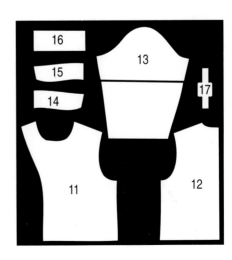

Trace the pattern pieces, and on the front and the back, follow **neckline A**. Compare the finished length of the blouse and the sleeve and lengthen or shorten the pattern, if necessary.

The fabric requirement is given on Page 86. If you have lengthened or shortened the pattern, take this into consideration before purchasing the fabric.

Fold the fabric, right sides together, and place the pattern pieces on the fabric, following the layout. Cut out the blouse.

Fabric 60" (152 cm) Wide

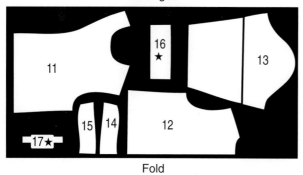

Fabric 45" (115 cm) Wide

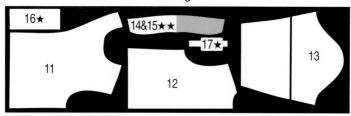

★ If making hemmed sleeves, eliminate pattern pieces 16 and 17.
★★ Unfold fabric and cut one of each, placed on fold.

Basic blouse.
Fabric: Cotton shirting

Use lightweight fusible interfacing and cut for the upper collar, front facings, and the cuffs, no layout is given. Fuse the interfacing to the wrong side of the upper collar, front facings, and the cuffs. For the front facings, it is easier to obtain a straight line if you first fold the facings on the fold lines to the wrong side and press. Place the interfacing along the crease and fuse in place. Overcast the outer edges of the facings.

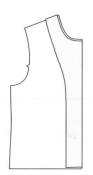

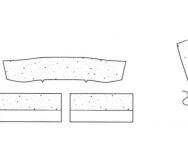
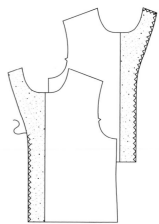

40

SHOULDER SEAMS

Sew the fronts to the back, right sides together, at the shoulder seams. Press the seam allowances toward the back.

COLLAR

On the upper collar, staystitch the back neckline on the seam line between the notches, see Sewing Terms on Page 17. Pin the upper collar to the under collar, right sides together, and sew the outer edge and the ends. Trim the corners and trim the under collar seam allowance so it is slightly narrower than the upper collar seam allowance. This procedure is called grading seams, see Sewing Terms on Page 17. Turn the collar right side out and press, rolling the seam slightly toward the under collar side.

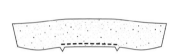
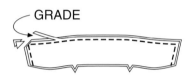
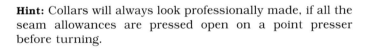

Hint: Collars will always look professionally made, if all the seam allowances are pressed open on a point presser before turning.

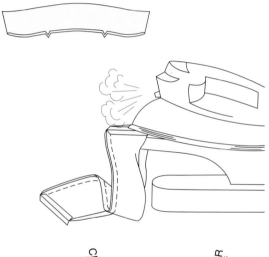

Pin the collar to the right side of neckline with the upper collar facing up; match the center backs, the notches to the shoulder seams, and the ends of collar to the center fronts. Pin only the under collar to the back neckline between the shoulder seams.

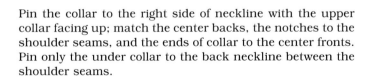

Fold the front facings on the fold lines to the right side over the collar, and the ends of facings extending 1/4" (6 mm) past the notches for shoulder seams. Pin the facing to the collar and neckline through all layers from front edges to shoulder seams. At the ends of facings, clip the seam allowance on the upper collar to the staystitching.

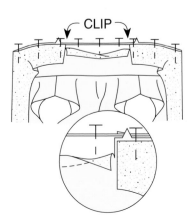

Sew the neckline through all layers the width of facing, continue to sew only the under collar to the back neckline, and sew through all layers the width of facing on the other side. Clip the seam allowances.

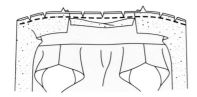

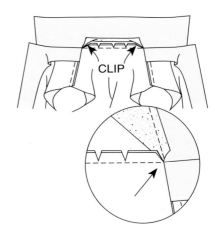

Turn the facings to the inside. Clip the neckline seam allowances at the ends of facings. Press the back neckline seam allowances toward the collar.

Fold under the seam allowance on the upper collar along the staystitching and pin to the neckline, covering the stitches. Sew close to the fold, or sew in place with hand stitches. Attach the facings to the shoulder seams with hand stitches.

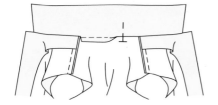 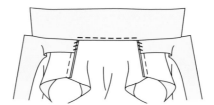

SLEEVE SLIT
On the sleeve, cut along the marked line to the dot. Pin the right side of the sleeve slit facing to the wrong side of the sleeve at the slit opening. Using a 1/8" (3 mm) seam allowance, sew from one end to 1/8" (3 mm) past the point of slit, lower the needle, turn the fabric and sew the other side; use a short stitch length at the point of slit.

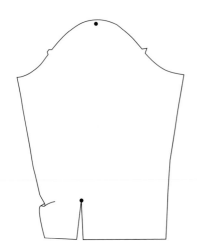 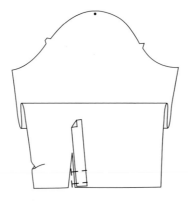 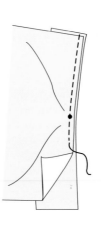

Press the seam allowances toward the slit facing. On the free edge of the slit facing, fold under the raw edge 1/4" (6 mm) and press. Fold the facing to the right side, and pin covering the stitches. Sew close to the folded edge. Trim the end of the slit facing even with the bottom of sleeve.

Fold the slit facing and the sleeve, right sides together, and sew across the top of facing at an angle, as illustrated.

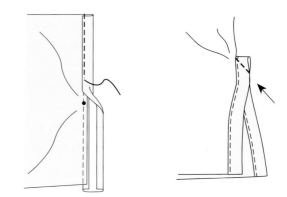

TUCKS

Make the tucks on the bottom edge of sleeve by folding the sleeve between the markings, right sides together, fold the tucks toward the slit and pin. On the front part of sleeve, turn the slit facing to the wrong side and pin; the facing extends on the back part of sleeve. Sew across the tucks and the facing to keep in place.

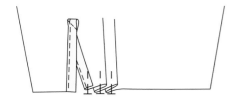

SEWING ON THE SLEEVES

Staystitch the cap of sleeve on seam line, between the notches, see Sewing Terms on Page 17. Pin the sleeve to the armhole, right sides together, matching the dot on sleeve to the shoulder seam, the notches on front and back, and the underarm edges even. Sew the armholes and press the seam allowances toward the sleeves.

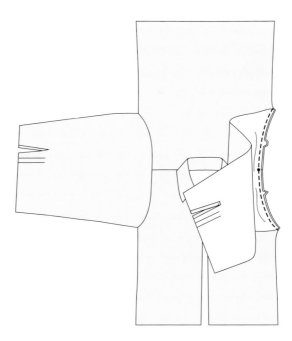

SIDE SEAMS

Pin the front to the back, right sides together, at the side seam and sleeve seam, matching the underarm seams. Sew from the bottom of blouse to the bottom of sleeve. Repeat for the other side.

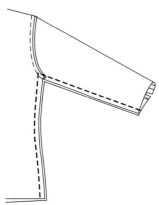

CUFFS

Fold each cuff on the fold line, right sides together, and sew the ends. Trim the corners and press the seam allowances open. Turn the cuffs right side out and press.

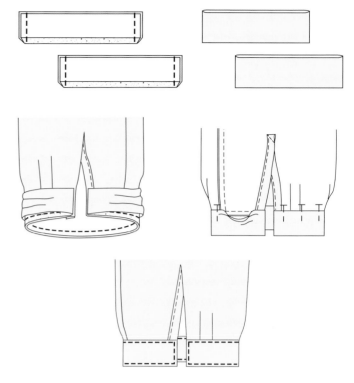

Pin one edge of the cuff (side with the interfacing) to the sleeve, right sides together, with the ends of cuff to the edges of slit. Sew on the cuff.

Press the seam allowances toward the cuff. Fold under the seam allowance of the inside cuff and pin, covering the stitches. Because the stitching will be done on the right side of the sleeve, transfer the pins to the outside cuffs. Topstitch on the cuff close to the seam. If desired, topstitch close to the outer edges of cuff. Repeat for the other cuff.

HEM

Overcast the bottom edge of blouse. At the bottom edge of front, fold the facing on the fold line to the right side and pin. Sew across the facing 1" (2.5 cm) above the bottom edge. Trim the hem on the facing. Turn the facing to the wrong side and press. Repeat for the other front.

Fold the 1" (2.5 cm) hem to the wrong side, press and pin. Sew close to the edge of hem.

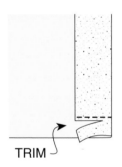

TRIM

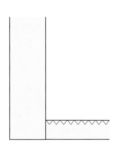

HEMMED SLEEVES

If making the blouse with short sleeves or the full length sleeves without cuffs, eliminate the instructions for the sleeve slit, tucks and cuffs. Overcast the bottom edges of sleeves. Hem the sleeves, using the same procedure as for the bottom edge of blouse.

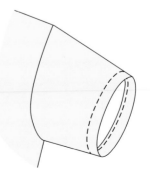

BUTTONHOLES AND BUTTONS

Mark the placements for buttonholes on the right front 1/2" (1.3 cm) from the front edge. Divide the front evenly into five and mark. Make four horizontal buttonholes and sew the buttons to the left front along the center front to match. If you have changed the length of the blouse, the buttonhole placements may need to be adjusted.

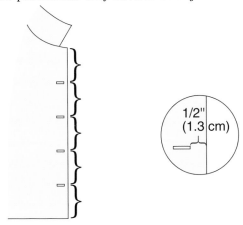

If making the long sleeves with cuffs, transfer the button-hole placement marked on the pattern to the front part of each cuff (end with tucks). Make the buttonholes and sew the buttons to the other ends of cuffs to match.

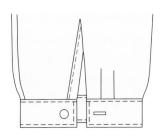

HIDDEN BUTTON CLOSURE

You can easily make the blouse with a hidden button closure. Disregard the instructions for the buttonholes above and follow these procedures:

You will need to make a placket for the buttonholes. Cut a piece of fabric 2 3/4" (7 cm) wide and 14" (35 cm) long. If you have changed the length of the blouse, you have to adjust the length of the placket.

Fold the placket lengthwise, wrong sides together, and press. Cut a piece of interfacing and fuse to half of the placket as shown.

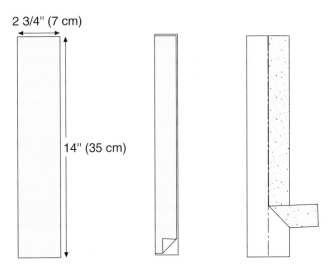

Fold the placket, right sides together, and stitch both ends. Trim the corners, turn right side out and press. Overcast the raw edges together.

Mark the placements for the top of the buttonholes 1/2" (1.3 cm) from the folded edge as follows:
The top placement 1/2" (1.3 cm) below the top edge, the bottom placement 1 1/2" (4 cm) above the bottom edge. Divide the distance between these two marks into three and mark the remaining two placements. Make 5/8" (1.5 cm) vertical buttonholes.

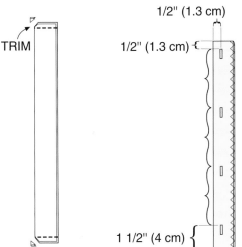

Place the placket on the right front facing with the folded edge 1/8" (2 mm) from the front edge and the top of the piece 3 1/2" (9 cm) below the neckline. Sew the placket to the facing only, along the overcasted edge of placket.

From the right side, sew through all layers at the top and the bottom of the placket and evenly between the buttonholes. Start the stitches 1/4" (6 mm) from the front edge and stitch for 3/4" (2 cm). Sew the buttons to the left front along the center front to match the buttonholes.

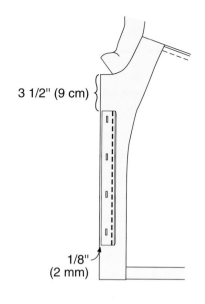

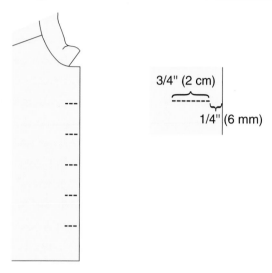

SPEED SEWING METHOD FOR COLLAR AND CUFFS

You can save a lot of time by using the following method for sewing the collar and cuffs to the blouse. It will not be as professional looking, because the seam allowances will show on the inside at the neckline and the cuffs. However, if you have a sewing machine that overcasts, or a serger (overlock) machine, this is a great method to use.

COLLAR
Sew the shoulder seams and the collar as described on Page 41, eliminating the staystitching on the collar.

Pin the collar to the right side of neckline with the upper collar facing up; match the center back, the notches to the shoulder seams, and the ends of collar to the center fronts.

Fold the front facings on the fold lines to the right side over the collar and the ends of facings extending 1/4" (6 mm) past the notches for the shoulder seams and pin. Sew the neckline through all layers. Clip the front neckline seam allowances and overcast the back neckline seam allowances together.

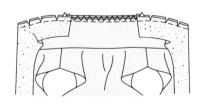

Turn the facings to the inside and press. Press the back neckline seam allowances toward the back and sew through the seam allowances and back close to the seam. Attach the facings to the shoulder seams.

CUFFS

The following method of finishing the sleeve slit and cuff is easier, faster and eliminates the sleeve slit facing. Cut the sleeve slit to the dot as marked on the pattern. On the slit, fold a 1/4" (6 mm) hem to the wrong side, fold as close as possible to the top of the slit, and press. Fold under the raw edge to make a double hem. Sew one side as far as you can, continue sewing to 1/8" (3 mm) past the slit, pivot, and sew the other side.

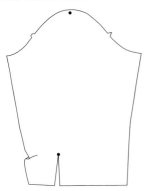 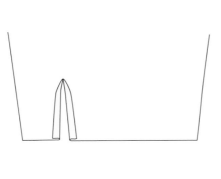 

Fold the slit and the sleeve, right sides together, and sew a small dart at the top of slit as illustrated.

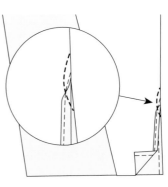

Sew the sleeve seam and the cuff as described previously. Sew gathering stitches on the bottom edge of sleeve on the seam line and again in the middle of the seam allowance.

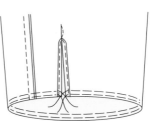

Pin the cuff (side with the interfacing) to the right side of the bottom edge of sleeve with all the raw edges together. On the back part of sleeve (smaller part) place the end of cuff even with the edge, place the other end of cuff 1/2" (1.3 cm) from the edge of slit. Pull up the gathering stitches to fit the cuff, adjusting the gathers evenly, and pin. Fold the extending edge of slit over the cuff and pin. Sew through all the layers.

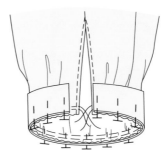 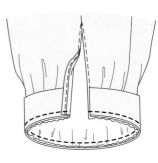

Trim the seam allowances and overcast together. Remove the gathering stitches. Turn the slit on the front part of sleeve to the inside.

 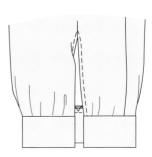

TRIM

BLOUSE WITH SCOOP NECKLINE AND FACING

This blouse has the neckline finished with a facing and can be made with the same sleeve variations as the basic blouse.

Use Master pattern pieces:

11. **Front**
12. **Back**
13. **Sleeve**
18. **Back Facing**
16. **Cuff** (if making long sleeves with cuffs)
17. **Sleeve Slit Facing** (if making long sleeves with cuffs)

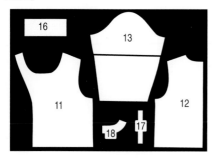

Trace the pattern pieces, and on the front and back, follow **neckline B**. Compare the length of the blouse and the sleeves given on Page 39, and lengthen or shorten the pattern, if necessary.

The fabric requirement is given on Page 86. If you have lengthened or shortened the pattern, take this into consideration before purchasing the fabric.

Fold the fabric, right sides together, and place the pattern pieces on the fabric, following the layouts. Cut out the pattern pieces.

Blouse with scoop neckline and facing.
Long gored skirt.
Fabric: Polyester georgette

FABRIC 45" (115 cm) WIDE
Selvages

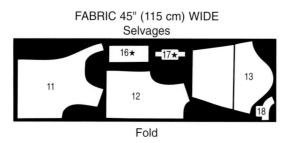

Fold

FABRIC 60" (152 cm) WIDE
Selvages

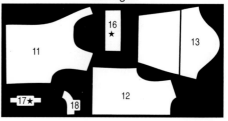

Fold

Cut interfacing for the front and back facings. Fuse the interfacing to the wrong side of the front and back facings. If making long sleeves with cuffs, cut interfacing for the cuffs and fuse to the wrong side.

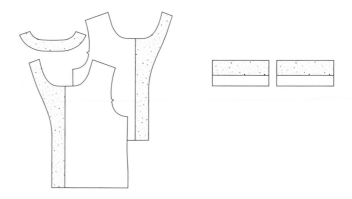

Sew the fronts to the back at the shoulder seams, as described on Page 41.

48

Sew the back facing to the front facings, right sides together, at the shoulder seams. Press the seam allowances toward the front facings. Overcast the outer edge of facings.

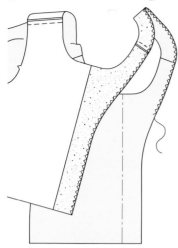

Fold the front facings on the fold lines to the right side and pin the neckline, matching the center back and the shoulder seams. Sew the neckline. Clip the seam allowances and trim the corners.

Understitch the neckline seam allowances to the facing; start and stop sewing as close as possible to the front edges, see Sewing Terms on Page 17. Fold the facings to the inside and press. Attach the facings to the shoulder seams with hand stitches.

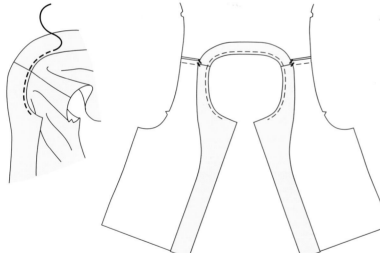

Continue to sew the blouse as previously described.

Mark the placements for buttonholes on the right front 1/2" (1.3 cm) from the front edge as follows: Mark the top buttonhole 1/2" (1.3 cm) below the neckline. Divide the remaining distance evenly into five. Make horizontal buttonholes and sew the buttons to the left front along the center front to match. If you have changed the length of the blouse, the buttonhole placements may need to be adjusted.

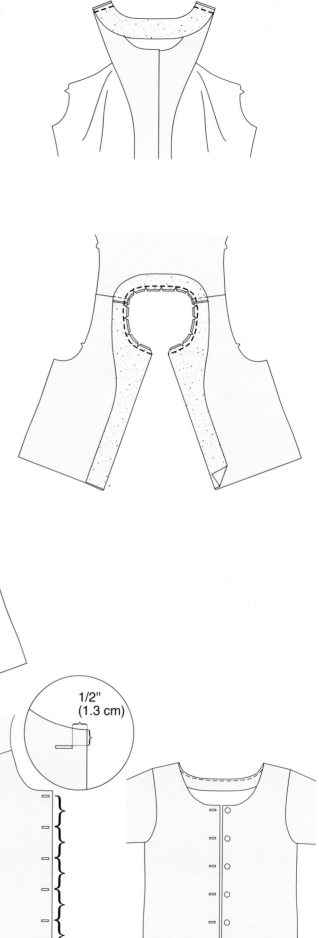

1/2"
(1.3 cm)

PULLOVER TOP WITH NECKLINE BINDING

You can easily make a pullover top, using the same pattern pieces as for the Blouse with Scoop Neckline, eliminating the back facing. Trace the pattern pieces, and on the front and the back, follow **neckline B**. On the front pattern piece, eliminate the facing and trace, **following the center front line**. Cut out the top, being sure to **place the front on the fold** of the fabric.

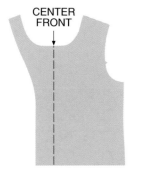

For the binding, cut a strip of fabric on the bias 1 3/8" (3.5 cm) wide and the following length:

XS - 25 3/4" (65.5 cm)
S - 26 1/2" (67.5 cm)
M - 27 3/8" (69.5 cm)
L - 28 1/4" (71.5 cm)
XL - 29" (73.5 cm)

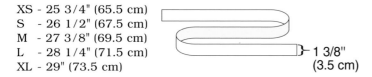

1 3/8" (3.5 cm)

Refer to Page 20, for cutting bias strips.

Make the ends angled to reduce the bulk in the joining seam. To trim the ends, measure and mark 1 3/8" (3.5 cm) from the ends of the binding, as illustrated. Draw lines from the marks to the corners. Trim the ends, following the lines.

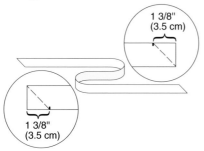

Sew the front to the back, right sides together, at the shoulder seams. Press the seam allowances toward the back.

Pin the ends of binding, right sides together, matching the seam lines, see illustration. Sew the ends together and press the seam allowances open. Trim the extending edges of the seam allowances.

Fold the binding in half lengthwise, wrong sides and the raw edges together, and press. Divide the binding and the neckline into fourths with pins.

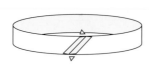
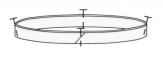
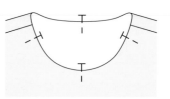

Pullover top with neckline binding.
Fabric: Printed polyester sheer

Pin the binding to the right side of neckline, matching the pins; place the seam at the back neckline. Sew the binding to the neckline and clip the seam allowances.

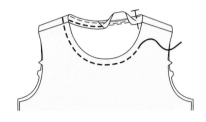

Understitch the neckline seam allowances to the binding, see Sewing Terms on Page 17. Trim the seam allowances close to the stitches.

TRIM

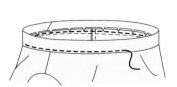 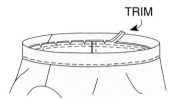

Fold the binding to the inside, press and pin. Sew close to the inner edge of the binding.

BLOUSE WITH SCOOP NECKLINE, BUTTON CLOSURE AND BINDING

Use the same pattern pieces as for the Blouse with Scoop Neckline, eliminating the back facing. Trace the pattern pieces, and on the front and the back, **follow neckline B**. Adjust the front pattern piece to make the front facing narrower; measure and draw a line 1 1/2" (4 cm) from the fold line. Cut out the blouse.

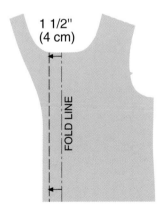

1 1/2" (4 cm)

FOLD LINE

For the binding, cut a strip of fabric on the bias 1 3/8" (3.5 cm) wide and the following length:

XS - 23 7/8" (60.5 cm)
S - 24 5/8" (62.5 cm)
M - 25 1/2" (64.5 cm)
L - 26 3/8" (67 cm)
XL - 27 1/8" (69 cm)

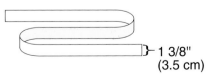

1 3/8" (3.5 cm)

Refer to Page 20, for cutting bias strips.

Blouse with scoop neckline, button closure and binding.
Fabric: Rayon gauze

Cut two pieces of fusible interfacing 1 1/2" (4 cm) wide and the length of the front edge. Fuse the interfacing to the wrong side of front facings, as shown. Overcast the outer edges of facings. Fold the front facings on the fold lines to the wrong side and press. Sew the shoulder seams as described previously.

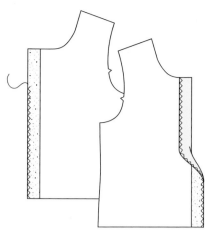

On the front neckline, mark the center fronts with pins. Divide the neckline between the pins into fourths and mark. Fold the front facings on the fold lines to the right side and pin to the neckline.

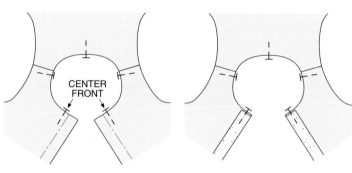

Fold the binding lengthwise, wrong sides and raw edges together, and press. Divide the binding into fourths with pins.

Pin the binding to the right side of the neckline, matching the pins and the ends of binding to the center fronts. Sew the binding to the neckline. Clip the seam allowances.

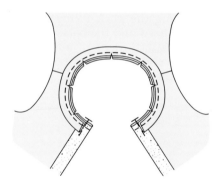

Turn the front facings to the wrong side. Understitch the neckline seam allowances to the binding, see Sewing Terms on Page 17. Trim the seam allowances close to the stitches. Fold the binding to the inside, press and pin. Sew close to the inner edge of binding.

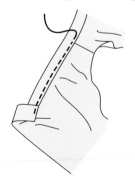 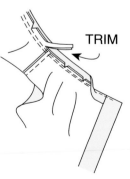 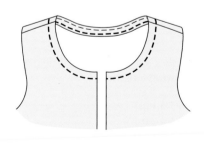

Continue to sew the blouse as previously described. If desired, after hemming the blouse, stitch the facings to the fronts 1 1/4" (3 cm) from the front edges.

Mark the placements for the top of vertical buttonholes on the right front along the center front as follows: The top mark 1/2" (1.3 cm) below the neckline. Divide the remaining distance evenly into five. Make the buttonholes and sew the buttons to the left front along the center front to match. If you have changed the length of the blouse, the buttonhole placements may need to be adjusted.

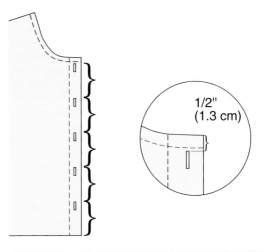

PULLOVER TOP WITH COLLAR AND SLIT

Top has a collar and a front slit with a facing and it can be made with short or long sleeves. Use the same pattern pieces as for the Basic Blouse. Trace the pattern pieces, and on the front and the back, follow **neckline A**. On the front pattern piece, trace, **following the center front line**.

To make the pattern piece for the front facing, trace the neckline, shoulders and center front. For the outer edge of facing, measure along center front 6" (15 cm) from the neckline and mark. On the shoulder, measure 2" (5 cm) from the neckline and mark. At the bottom of facing, mark 1" (2.5 cm) from the center front. Draw the facing line and round the corners, as illustrated.

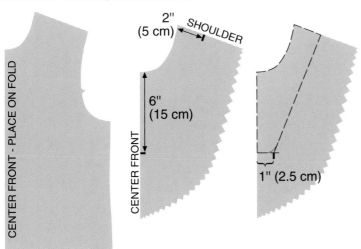

Cut out the top and be sure to **place the center fronts of the front and the front facing on the fold** of the fabric.

Cut interfacing for the upper collar and the front facing and fuse to the wrong side. On the interfaced side of front facing, mark a 4 3/4" (12 cm) long line along the center front for the slit. Overcast the outer edge of facing. Mark the center front on the right side of front, using a water soluble pen or basting stitches.

Pullover top with collar and slit. Side hemline slits.
Basic Pants.
Fabric: Crinkled polyester suiting

53

Pin the facing to the front, right sides together, matching the center front lines. Using a short stitch length, sew 1/8" (3 mm) on each side of the line marked, pivoting at the end of line. Cut between the stitching lines from the neckline to the bottom of stitches. Turn the facing to the wrong side and press.

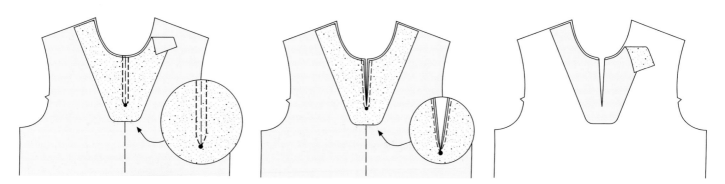

Sew the shoulder seams and the collar, as previously described. Pin the collar to the right side of neckline, with the upper collar facing up, matching the center back, the notches to the shoulder seams, and the ends of collar to the facing seams. Sew the collar to the neckline through all the layers.

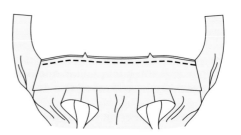

Fold the front facings to the right side over the collar with the ends of facing extending 1/4" (6 mm) past the notches for the shoulder seams and pin. Sew both sides of the facing, following the stitches for sewing on the collar. Clip the curved front neckline seam allowances and trim the corners. Overcast the back neckline seam allowances together.

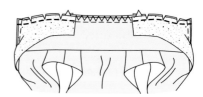

Turn the facing to the inside and press. Attach the facings to the shoulder seams.

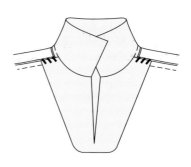

If desired, topstitch 1/4" (6 mm) from the outer edge of collar and slit, as shown. Continue to sew as previously described.

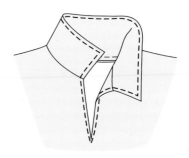

POCKETS

The Master Pattern piece 19 includes three different styles of pockets. The pocket with the straight and the angled bottom edge is sized for a breast pocket. If using one breast pocket, it should be placed on the left side of the garment. The lower pocket with the rounded bottom edge should be placed below the waist. These pockets can be sewn to blouses, T-shirts, tops, and dresses. The placement for the breast pocket is marked on the T-shirt and the blouse pattern. It is much easier to sew the pockets to the garment before sewing any other pieces together.

BREAST POCKET

Trace Master Pattern piece 19, following the lines for the pocket style you have chosen. Cut out the pocket. Cut a piece of lightweight fusible interfacing the width and length of the pocket facing and fuse to the wrong side of the pocket facing. Overcast the raw edge of the pocket facing. Fold the pocket facing on the fold line to the wrong side and press.

Fold the pocket facing on the fold line to the right side and sew each side the width of facing. Trim the corners and the facing seam allowances. Turn the facing to the wrong side. Fold under the seam allowances of the pocket; first fold the bottom seam allowance and press, then the sides. Sew across the pocket close to the edge of facing.

Pin the pocket to the garment at the placement marked, or at placement desired, and stitch close to the side and bottom edges. Reinforce the top corners of pocket by stitching triangles, as shown.

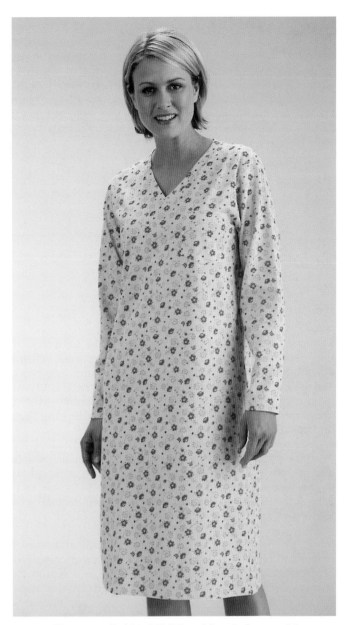

Sleepwear T-shirt, 26" (66 cm) length from waist.
V-neck. Breast pocket.
Fabric: Cotton jersey

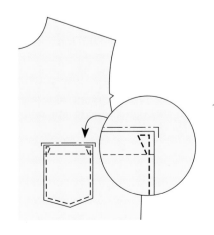

55

LOWER POCKETS

This pocket can be sewn to a jacket, dress, tunic, pants or shorts. Trace Master Pattern piece 19, following the lines for the lower pocket. Cut out the pocket. Cut a piece of lightweight fusible interfacing the width and the length of pocket facing and fuse to the wrong side of pocket facing. Overcast the raw edge of pocket facing. Fold the pocket facing on the fold line to the wrong side and press.

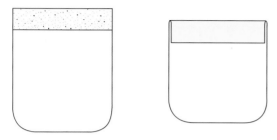

Fold the pocket facing on the fold line to the right side and pin. Sew each side the width of facing and continue staystitching around the pocket on seam line, see Sewing Terms on Page 17. Trim the corners and the facing seam allowances. Sew easing stitches in the middle of seam allowance on the curved edges of pocket, see Sewing Terms on Page 17.

Turn the facing to the wrong side. Pull up the easing stitches and fold the seam allowances along the staystitching to the wrong side and press. Sew across the pocket close to the edge of facing. For a dressier look, blind hem the facing, see Hems on Page 18.

Mark the pocket placements. The general rule for the placement of lower pockets is 3" (8 cm) below the waist and centered between the center front and the side seams. Sew the pocket to the garment as described for the Breast pocket on Page 55.

BUTTON AND BUTTONHOLE ON POCKET

Buttons and buttonholes add detail and can also prevent the pockets from gapping, when using soft fabrics. If making a pocket with a buttonhole and button, add 3/8" (1 cm) to the width of the pocket facing before cutting the pocket.

Make the pocket as described previously. Before sewing the pocket to the garment, make a buttonhole in the center of the pocket 3/8" (1 cm) below the top edge.

After the garment is completed, sew a button to the garment under the buttonhole. It is a good idea to place a small piece of interfacing on the wrong side for reinforcement. Sew the button through the garment and the interfacing and trim any excess interfacing.

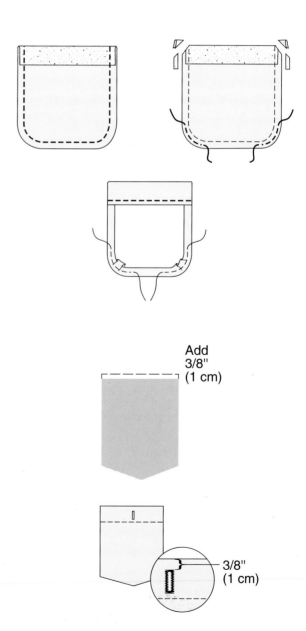

Add 3/8" (1 cm)

3/8" (1 cm)

The Master Pattern includes pants in two lengths and shorts. They are easy to make and comfortable to wear. The pants are pull-on style with elastic in a casing at the waist and they have straight legs. The pants can be made with or without pockets in the side seams.

For the pants, we recommend light to medium weight woven and firm knit fabrics. Use cotton, cotton types, sheeting, challis, rayon and blends, twill, French terry, flannel, double knit and jersey. Because the pants are pull-on style and have extra fullness at the waist, it is best to choose soft fabrics. When choosing prints or stripes, it is a good idea to drape the fabric around you and look in the mirror to check the effect. A large print in a bold color can make you look heavier, while the same print in soft muted colors may not.

BASIC PANTS
Use Master Pattern pieces:
 20. Pants Front
 21. Pants Back

For pockets, use pattern pieces:
 22. Side Pocket Method I
 23. Side Pocket Method II

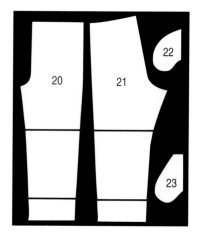

Basic pants with pockets.
Fabric: Rayon suiting

Trace the pattern pieces. The pattern includes 1/4" (6 mm) seam allowances and the seam allowances will be pressed to one side. If you wish to press the seam allowances open, add 3/8" (1 cm) to the pattern at the outside and the inside leg seams, to allow for 5/8" (1.5 cm) seam allowances.

The pattern allows for a 1 3/8" (3.5 cm) casing at the waist and 1" (2.5 cm) wide elastic is used. If you wish to have a wider elastic, add to the waist, twice the difference between the widths of the elastics. For example, if using a 1 1/2" (4 cm) wide elastic, add 1" (2.5 cm) to the waist edges on the front and the back pattern pieces.

The finished inside leg seams are:
PANTS - 30" (76 cm) for all sizes.
CROPPED PANTS - 25" (63 cm) for all sizes.
SHORTS - 9" (23 cm) for all sizes.

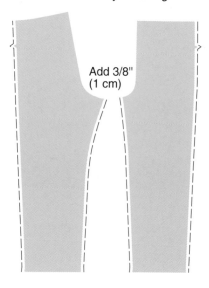

Add 3/8" (1 cm)

Compare your length to the measurement above and adjust the length, if necessary. Refer to Page 8.

CROTCH DEPTH

The crotch depth on the Master pattern allows for the following body measurements:

XS	S	M	L	XL
9 3/4"	10 1/2"	11 1/2"	12 1/4"	13"
25 cm	27 cm	29 cm	31 cm	33 cm

Measure your crotch depth, following Page 7. Compare your measurement to the above measurement and lengthen or shorten the pattern, using the shorten and lengthen line marked on the pattern. Make sure to lengthen or shorten the same amount on the front and the back pattern pieces.

Lengthen

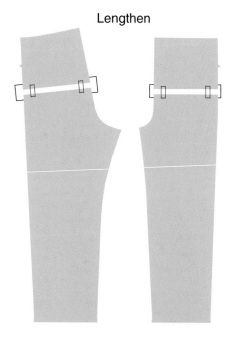

Shorten

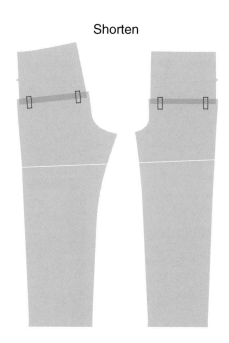

Compare your hip measurement to the measurement given on Page 6 and to the finished measurement of pants given on the front pattern piece. If you need to add or deduct to the hips, divide the difference into four and add or deduct this amount on the front and the back at the outside leg seams. Be sure to taper the adjustments to obtain smooth lines.

Deduct   Deduct

Add   Add

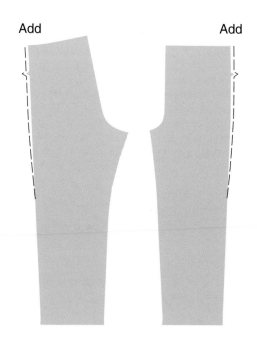

58

The finished widths of legs at bottom edge are:

PANTS						CROPPED PANTS				
XS	S	M	L	XL		XS	S	M	L	XL
17 1/4"	18 1/4"	19 1/4"	20 1/4"	21 1/4"		18"	19"	20"	21"	22"
44 cm	46 cm	48 cm	51 cm	54 cm		45 cm	48 cm	51 cm	53 cm	56 cm

The width of the legs can be adjusted to your personal preference. Compare the width of legs desired to the measurement given and divide this difference into four. The adjustment has to be made on both the inside and the outside leg seams and on both the front and the back pattern pieces. At the bottom of the legs, mark inside the original pattern line to decrease the width, or mark outside the original line to increase the width. Now draw lines from the bottom of the legs to the line for shorts.

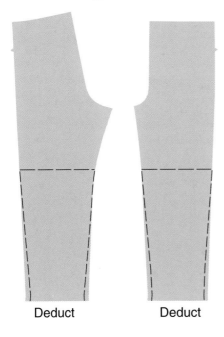

Deduct   Deduct

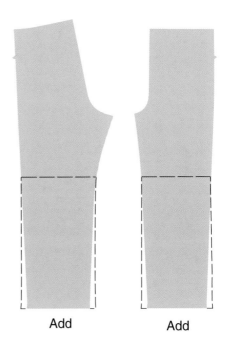

Add   Add

CUTTING

Make any necessary adjustments on the pattern pieces before cutting. The fabric requirement is given on Page 87. If you changed the length of the pants, or made any other adjustments, take this into consideration before purchasing the fabric.

Fold the fabric double, right sides together. Place the pattern pieces on the fabric, following the layouts. Be sure to follow the grain of fabric lines, as it will ensure that the pants hang correctly. Cut out the pants.

FABRIC 60" (152 cm) WIDE
Selvages

[Layout showing pieces: 21, 20, and 22 or 23]

Fold

FABRIC 45" (115 cm) WIDE
Selvages

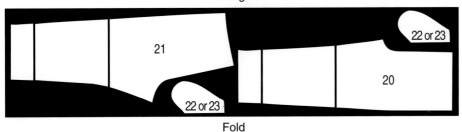

[Layout showing pieces: 21, 20, and 22 or 23]

Fold

PANTS WITHOUT POCKETS

Pin the fronts to the backs, right sides together, and sew the outside leg seams from the bottom edge to the waist. Press the seam allowances toward the back.

Sew the inside leg seams from the bottom of the legs to the crotch. Press the seam allowances toward the back. To ensure that the legs will not twist, it is important to sew all the seams in the same direction.

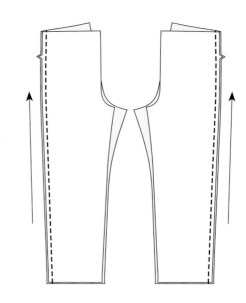

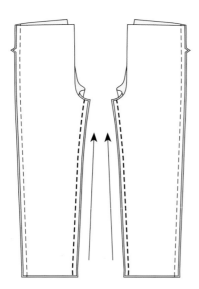

Turn one leg right side out. Place this leg inside the other leg, right sides together. Pin the center front and the center back seams together, matching the inside leg seams and the waist edges even. Sew from the front waist to the back waist. Turn the pants right side out.

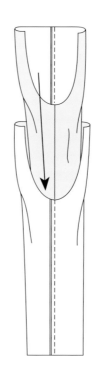

WAIST

For the waist, cut one piece of 1" (2.5 cm) wide elastic the following length:

XS	S	M	L	XL
22"	24"	27"	30"	34"
56 cm	61 cm	68 cm	76 cm	86 cm

Or measure the elastic around your waist so it feels comfortable, and add 3/8" (1 cm) for the seam allowance. If the elastic is too tight, it will have a tendency to roll. The length of the elastic depends on the type of elastic and your personal preference.

Overlap the ends of the elastic 3/8" (1 cm) and pin. Lower the needle into the middle of the elastic and sew to the edge, backstitch to the other edge, and again sew to the middle. Use a three-step zigzag or a zigzag stitch.

To check the fit of the pants, try on the pants and be sure to wear shoes. Place the elastic over the pants at your waist. Fold up the hems at the bottom of legs and pin. Stand in front of a mirror and pull the pants up until the crotch feels comfortable and the legs hang straight.

Pants have extra fullness at the waist, if you wish, some of the fullness can be removed from the waist and the hips. Be sure not to "over fit" the waist, the pants should slide easily over the hips. Pin the extra fullness at the outside leg seams.

Remove the pants and transfer the markings to the wrong side of the pants. Using a curved ruler and a water soluble pen, draw the new stitching line and taper this line for a smooth seam. Make the same adjustment on both sides. Sew on the new lines and trim the excess fabric.

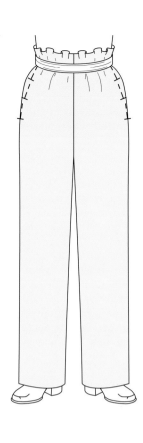

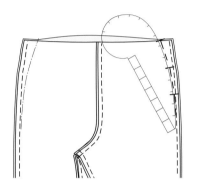 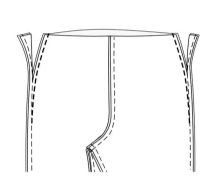

To check the fit of the waist, try on the pants and use the same procedures for fitting as above. Mark the **top edge of the elastic** with pins or a water soluble pen.

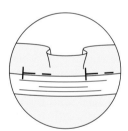

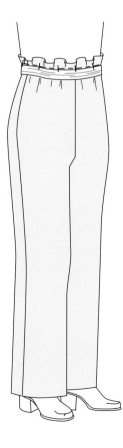

Remove the pants and fold the pants in half, matching the outside leg seams and the raw edges even at waist. Measure 1 3/8" (3.5 cm) above the marks and trim any excess fabric. Note: If the measurement from the marks is less than 1 3/8" (3.5 cm), use a narrower elastic for the waist.

1 3/8" (3.5 cm)

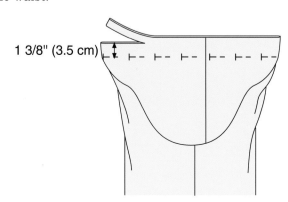

Overcast the raw edge of waist. Fold 1 3/8" (3.5 cm) to the wrong side for the casing and press. Place the elastic inside the casing and using a zipper foot, sew close to the elastic, being sure not to catch the elastic with your stitches. Sew, without stretching the elastic, when needed, lower the needle and gently pull the elastic from the sewn casing so the fabric and elastic are flat when sewing.

Distribute the gathers evenly by stretching the elastic repeatedly. To keep the elastic from rolling, sew across the width of the elastic through all layers, at the center front, center back and the outside leg seams.

Another method of finishing the waist is to sew the casing first and thread the elastic into the casing. Stitch the casing seam close to edge and leave a 2" (5 cm) opening for inserting the elastic. Hook a safety pin to one end of the elastic and insert into the casing through the opening. Overlap the ends of elastic and sew together. Finish sewing the casing seam.

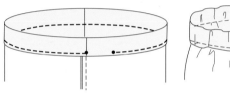 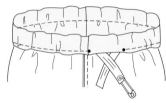 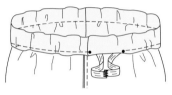 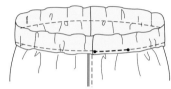

SERGER METHOD
The serger method for applying the waist elastic is easy and keeps the elastic from rolling.

Trim the waist 3/8" (1 cm). Sew the elastic into a circle as previously described. Divide the elastic into fourths and mark. Pin the elastic to the wrong side of waist, matching the marks to the center front, center back and the outside leg seams; place the edge of elastic even with the edge of fabric. Using the serger (overlock) machine, sew over the edges of elastic and waist, stretching the elastic to fit, be careful not to cut the elastic.

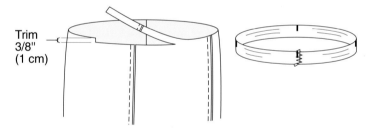

Trim 3/8" (1 cm)

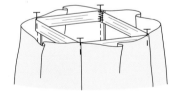 

Fold the casing to the wrong side and sew close to the edge, stretching the elastic to fit fabric. Use a longer than medium stitch length. If you wish, you can add another row of stitches in the middle of the casing.

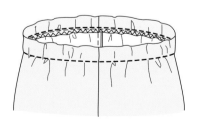

HEMMING
Overcast the bottom edges of legs. Measure and fold 1" (2.5 cm) hems to the wrong side, press and pin. Hem, see Page 18.

POCKETS IN SIDE SEAMS

Pockets can be added to the pants or the shorts. The pockets have to be sewn to the pants, before sewing any other seams. There are several methods of applying the pockets to the side seams. We will show two methods. Method I can be made completely on the serger (overlock) machine. Method II has more sewing steps, but the pockets stay in place better.

EASY METHOD I

Use pattern piece 22 and cut four pockets. Pin a pocket to each front at the outside leg seams, right sides together, matching the notches and sew. Press pockets away from pants. Sew the remaining pockets to the backs, using the same procedure.

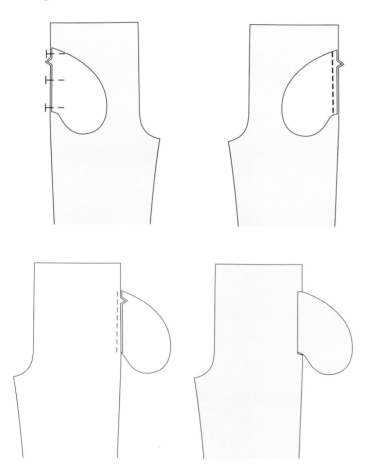

Basic blouse, lengthened to 26" (66 cm) from waist.
Side hemline slits. Hemmed sleeves.
Pants with pockets.
Pullover top with neckline binding.
Fabric: Linen. Top - polyester georgette

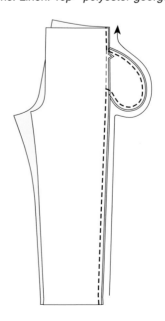

Pin the front to the back, right sides together, at the outside leg seams and pin the pockets, right sides together. Start at the bottom of the leg and sew to the pocket, pivot, sew around the pocket, pivot, and sew to the waist. Press the pocket toward the front. Continue to sew the pants as previously described for Pants without pockets.

METHOD II

Use pattern piece 23 and cut four pockets. Cut two pieces of fusible interfacing, following the cutting line marked on the pattern. Fuse the interfacing to the wrong side of one pair of pockets. Transfer the stitching lines to the interfaced side of the pockets.

Pin the interfaced pocket to the front, right sides together, matching the notches and sew, following the stitching line marked; use a short stitch length at the corners. Clip to the corners of the stitches, see illustration. Turn the pocket to the wrong side and press, rolling the seam slightly to the pocket side. Topstitch close to the edges of pocket opening.

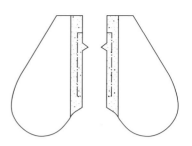

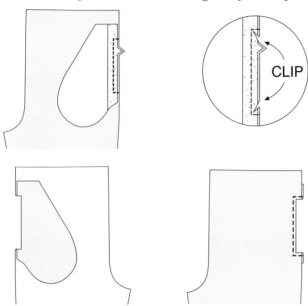

Pin the other pocket to the pocket on front, right sides together, matching the raw edges. Sew the pockets together and overcast the seam allowances together.

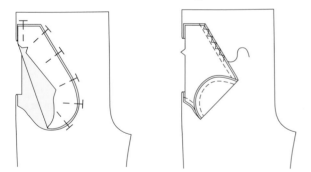

Secure the pocket to the outside leg seam by sewing close to the edge and baste the pocket to the front close to the top edge of pocket. Sew the other pocket to the other front using the same procedure. Continue to sew the pants as previously described for Pants without pockets.

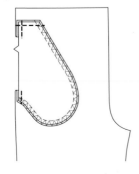

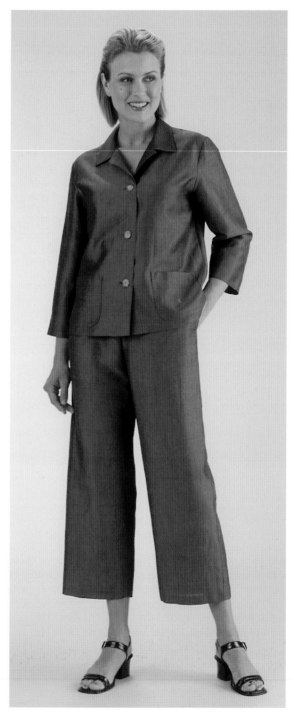

Basic blouse. Lower pockets. Three quarter length sleeves.
Cropped pants with pockets.
Fabric: Linen blend suiting

DRAWSTRING WAIST

You can make pants or shorts with a drawstring instead of elastic at the waist. Use a purchased drawstring or make a self fabric tie. Sew the pants, following the Basic Pants, except for the waist.

Overcast the raw edge of waist. On the front, mark two 5/8" (1.5 cm) vertical buttonholes 1 5/8" (4 cm) below the raw edge of waist and 5/8" (1.5 cm) on each side of the center front seam. Place a piece of fusible interfacing on the wrong side, under the buttonhole placements, and fuse in place. Make the buttonholes.

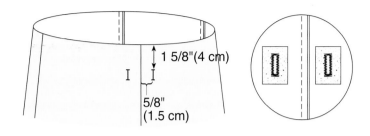

For the casing, fold the waist 1 3/8" (3.5 cm) to the wrong side and press. Stitch close to the edge of casing. Insert the drawstring into the casing through the buttonholes.

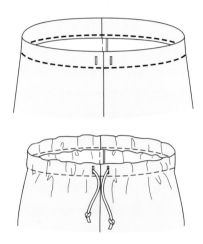

SELF FABRIC TIE

If you wish to make a tie from the self fabric, cut a strip of fabric 2" (5 cm) wide and to determine the length, measure your waist and add 25" (65 cm). The tie may have to be cut in two pieces.

If the tie was cut in two pieces, sew the pieces together, and press the seam allowances open. Fold the tie in half lengthwise, right sides together, and sew the ends and the long edge, leaving an opening in the center for turning. Trim the corners.

To turn the tie right side out, use the rubber part of a pencil and push the finished end inside the tie and out through the opening. Repeat for the other end of tie. Press the tie, fold under the edges of the opening and sew together close to edges.

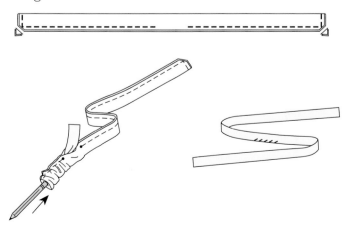

T-shirt. V-neck.
Shorts, shortened 4" (10 cm). Drawstring waist.
Fabric: T-shirt - cotton interlock. Shorts - seersucker.

SKIRTS

The Master Pattern includes a straight pull-on skirt and an eight gore skirt. Both skirts have elastic in a casing at the waist and are very easy to make. By using different fabrics and changing the length, you can make completely different looks.

For the skirts, we recommend light to medium weight woven or firm knit fabrics. Use cotton, cotton types, linen, sheeting, lightweight soft denim, rayon and blends, such as challis, silk and silk like fabrics. Use firm knits such as jersey, matte jersey, and double knits.

The finished length of the skirts are 26" (66 cm). Compare this length to the length you wish to have and lengthen or shorten the pattern, if necessary. The finished measurement of the skirt at the fullest part of hip is given on the pattern piece.

The skirt patterns include 1/4" (6 mm) seam allowances and the seam allowances will be pressed to one side. If you wish to press the seam allowances open, add 3/8" (1 cm) to the side seam to allow for 5/8" (1.5 cm) seam allowances.

Add 3/8" (1 cm)

Straight skirt. T-shirt with Mock turtleneck.
Fabric: Skirt - Rayon-poly tweed. Top - Polyester interlock.

STRAIGHT SKIRT

Trace pattern piece 24. Compare the finished length of skirt, given above, to the length of skirt you want. Shorten or lengthen the pattern piece if needed.

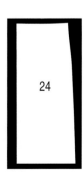

24

For fabric requirements, see Page 87. If you shortened or lengthened the pattern, take this into consideration before purchasing the fabric.

Place the pattern pieces on the fabric, following the layout and cut out the skirt.

FABRIC 45" (115 cm) WIDE Sizes: XS-S
FABRIC 60" (152 cm) WIDE All Sizes

Fold

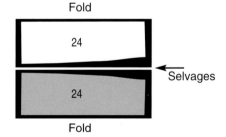

Selvages

FABRIC 45" (115 cm) WIDE Sizes: M-L-XL

Fold

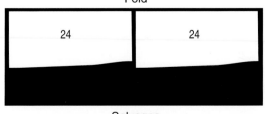

Selvages

Sew the skirt pieces, right sides together, at the side seams.

Finish the waist, following the same instructions as for the Pants on Pages 60 and 62.

Overcast the bottom edge of the skirt. Fold 1" (2.5 cm) hem to the wrong side and press. Hem the skirt, refer to Page 18.

LONG STRAIGHT SKIRT WITH HEMLINE SLIT

A long straight skirt will need a hemline slit in one or both side seams.

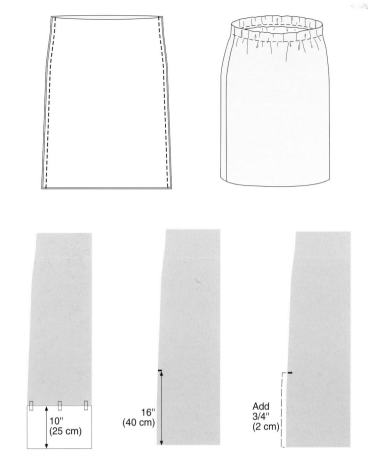

Make the following adjustment on pattern piece 24. For a finished length of 36" (91 cm), lengthen the pattern 10" (25 cm) at the bottom edge. Mark the position for the top of slit at the side seam 16" (40 cm) above the bottom edge. To make the facing for the slit, add 3/4" (2 cm) to the side seam, from the mark for the top of slit to the bottom of the skirt, this will allow for 1" (2.5 cm) wide slit facings.

When sewing the side seam, start to sew 1/4" (6 mm) below the top edge of the slit facing and sew to the waist. Clip the seam allowances above the facing to the stitches. If you wish to have the slit only on one side, trim the facings on the other side seam and sew the side seam from the bottom edge to the waist.

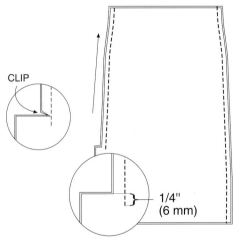

Overcast the bottom edge of skirt and the slit facings. Fold the 1" (2.5 cm) slit facings to the wrong side and press. Fold the slit facings on the creases to the right side and sew across the width of facings 1" (2.5 cm) above the bottom edge. Trim the hems on the facings. Turn the facings to the wrong side and press. Fold the 1" (2.5 cm) hem to the wrong side, press and pin. Sew close to the edges of hem, slit facings and across the top of slit as shown. Or if you prefer, blind hem the slit facings and the bottom edge, see Hems, Page 18.

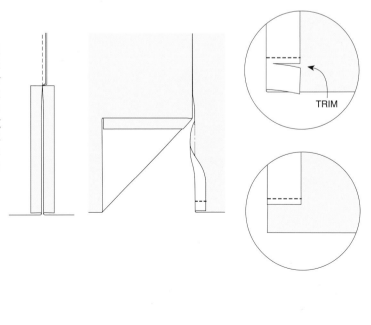

LINED SKIRTS

If you are making a skirt from sheer fabric, it is best to line the skirt with a fabric that will compliment the sheer. Cut the lining the same as the skirt. Sew the side seams of the skirt and the lining separately. Pin the skirt and the lining, wrong sides together, at the waist, matching the side seams and overcast the waist edges together, or stitch together to keep in place. Continue to sew the skirt as previously described. Hem the lining to be 1/2"-1" (1.3 cm-2.5 cm) shorter than the skirt.

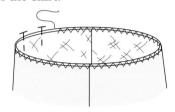

SKIRT WITH RUFFLE

A ruffle can be added to the bottom edge of the short straight skirt. To add a ruffle, cut two pieces of fabric 2"-5" (5 cm-13 cm) wide and the following length:

XS	S	M	L	XL
30"	32 1/2"	35"	37 1/2"	40"
76 cm	82 cm	89 cm	95 cm	102 cm

Sew the two ruffle pieces, right sides together. Finish one edge with a double hem as follows: Fold 1/2" (1.3 cm) to wrong side, and press. Fold under the raw edge to make a double hem and stitch. Divide the other edge of ruffle into fourths and mark with a water soluble pen. Sew gathering stitches 1/4" (6 mm) from the raw edge and again in the middle of seam allowance.

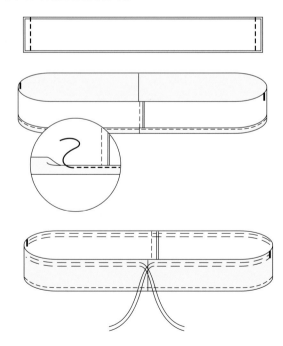

Skirt with ruffle at bottom edge.
Basic T-shirt.
Fabric: Skirt - rayon georgette. T-shirt - cotton interlock.

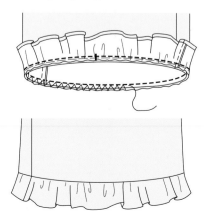

Pin the ruffle to the bottom edge of skirt, right sides together, matching the seams, and the other marks to the center front and the center back. Pull up the gathering stitches to fit the skirt, adjusting the gathers evenly and pin. Stitch and overcast the raw edges together.

GORED SKIRT

The gored skirt has eight gores, is fitted over the hips, and flares to the hemline.

Trace pattern piece 25. Compare the finished length of skirt, given on Page 66, and adjust the length if necessary.

The measurement of the finished skirt at the fullest part of the hip is given on the pattern piece. If you wish to change the size of the skirt; the following is the easiest way to adjust the pattern: Decide on the amount of adjustment needed and divide by eight; this is the amount you will add or deduct. Cut the skirt pattern piece apart on the center line. To deduct width, overlap the cut edges. To add width, place a piece of paper under the pattern piece, spread the pieces apart. Tape the pieces in place.

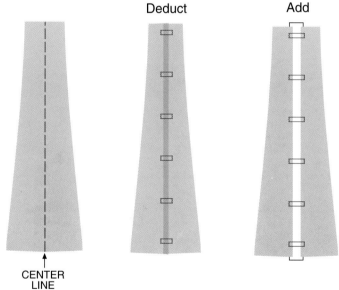

Deduct

Add

CENTER
LINE

*Blouse with scoop neckline, button closure and binding.
Side hemline slits.
Gored skirt.
Fabric: Polyester crepe*

For easier cutting, trace the pattern piece two or four times. Place the pattern pieces on the fabric, following the layouts. Cut out the skirt.

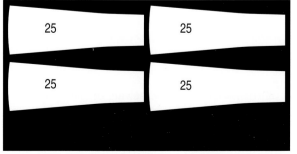

FABRIC 45" (115 cm) WIDE
Selvages

| 25 | 25 |
| 25 | 25 |

Fold

FABRIC 60" (152 cm) WIDE
Selvages

| 25 | 25 |
| 25 | 25 |

Fold

Sew the eight gores, right sides together, at all the panel seams. Press the seam allowances to one side. Or if desired, press the seam allowances open and topstitch all seams 1/8" (3 mm) on each side of the seam.

Finish the waist, following the same instructions as for the Pants on Pages 60 and 62.

Overcast the bottom edge of skirt. Fold the hem to the wrong side, press and pin. Hem the skirt, refer to Page 18.

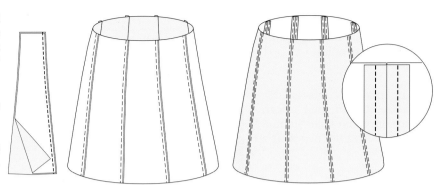

LONG GORED SKIRT

To make a long gored skirt, lengthen pattern piece 25 at the bottom edge, add 10" (25 cm) for a 36" (91 cm) long skirt. Continue the panel seams to make the skirt have more flare, see illustration.

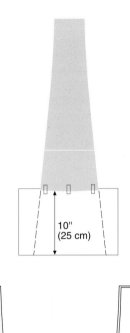

10"
(25 cm)

GUSSETS

Gussets can be added to the gored skirt at all the panel seams, they will make the bottom of the skirt have more flare. You will need to make a pattern piece for the gusset. Draw a line 15" (38 cm) long. Draw a perpendicular line and mark 4 1/2" (11 cm) on each side of the line. Connect the points, making a triangle.

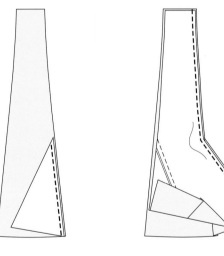

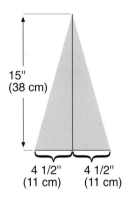

15"
(38 cm)

4 1/2"   4 1/2"
(11 cm)   (11 cm)

Cut eight gussets, the center line is the grain of fabric.

Pin one gusset to one skirt panel, right sides together, matching bottom edges and sew to the top of the gusset. Sew the other gussets to the other skirt panels, being sure to sew the gussets to the same side of all the skirt panels.

Sew all the panels, together, sewing the side with the gusset to the side without a gusset. Finish the skirt as previously described and hem the skirt with a narrow hem, see Hems on Page 18.

DRESS AND TUNIC

You can make a pattern for a dress or a tunic from the T-shirt or the blouse pattern by adding length. To make a dress with the finished length of 26" (66 cm) from the waist, add 20 1/2" (52 cm) to the bottom of both the front and the back pattern pieces; if you wish the finished length to be 36" (91 cm) from the waist, add 30 1/2" (77 cm). These measurements allow for a 1" (2.5 cm) hem.

To make a tunic with a finished length of 15 1/2" (39 cm) from the waist, add 10" (25 cm) to the bottom of both the front and the back. These measurements allow for a 1" (2.5 cm) hem.

To add length, extend the center line and the side seams the amount needed and draw the new bottom edge. Repeat for the back. If you wish to add side hemline slits, refer to Page 73.

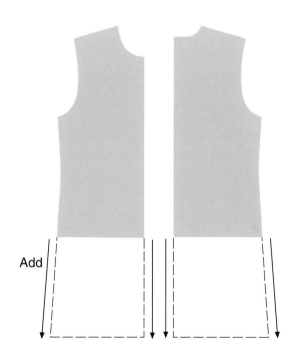

Add

Pullover top with neckline binding. Dress 36" (91 cm) length from waist. Back ties. Side hemline slit. Fabric: Rayon georgette

BACK TIES

Ties can be added to the side seams of a tunic or a dress and tied together at the center back for a slimmer silhouette.

Cut two strips of fabric 2" (5 cm) wide and the following length:

XS	S	M	L	XL
23"	24"	25"	26"	27"
58 cm	61 cm	63 cm	66 cm	68 cm

Fold each tie double lengthwise, right sides together, and sew one end and the long edge. Trim the corners.

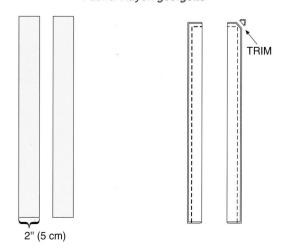

TRIM

2" (5 cm)

To turn the tie right side out, use the rubber part of a pencil and push the finished end inside the tie to the open end. Press the tie and if desired, topstitch close to the edges.

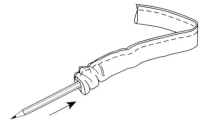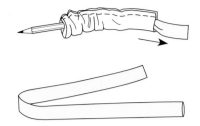

For the tie placement, transfer the mark for the natural waist on the back pattern piece to the side seams. Before sewing the side seams of the dress or the tunic, pin the ties to the right side of the back at the placements marked. Sew across ties.

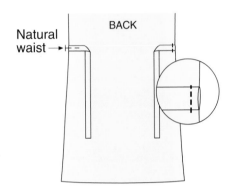

CENTER SEAMS

Center front and center back seams can easily be added to a T-shirt or a pullover top.

Add seam allowances to the front and the back pattern pieces at the center front and the center back. If you wish to press the seam allowances to one side, add 1/4" (6 mm) seam allowance; add 5/8" (1.5 cm), if you prefer to press the seam allowances open. When cutting out the garment, cut two fronts and two backs. Sew these seams first, then proceed as described previously.

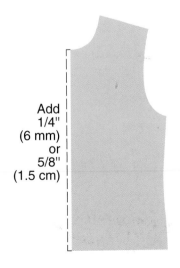

Add 1/4" (6 mm) or 5/8" (1.5 cm)

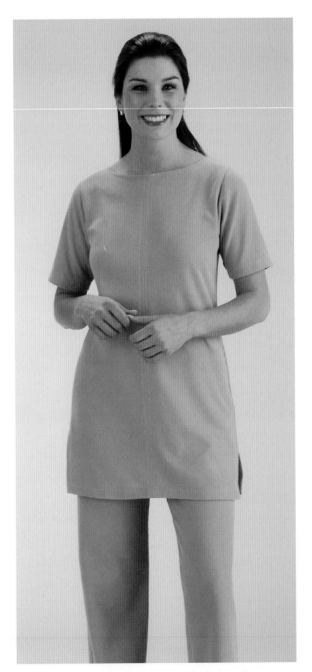

Top with boat neckline. Tunic length.
Center seams. Side hemline slits.
Basic pants.
Fabric: Cotton poly textured knit

SIDE HEMLINE SLITS

Side hemline slits can be added to T-shirts, blouses and tunics. Slits can be from 2" (5 cm) to 7" (18 cm) long. If you wish to have side hemline slits on a dress with 36" (91 cm) length from the waist, the slit should be approximately 16" (40 cm). Generally, the shorter the garment, the shorter the slit should be.

Mark the position for the top of the slit at the side seams on both the front and the back pattern pieces. To allow for 1" (2.5 cm) wide slit facings, add 3/4" (2 cm) to the side seams from the mark to the bottom edge.

Sew the side seam, starting 1/4" (6 mm) below the top of the slit facing. Clip the seam allowances above the slit facing to the stitches.

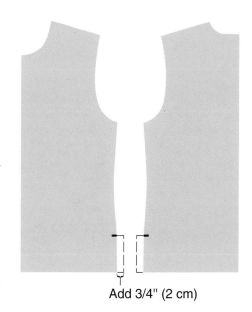

Add 3/4" (2 cm)

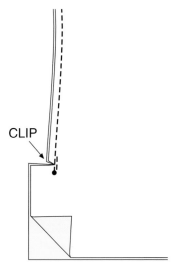

CLIP

Overcast the raw edges of the bottom edge and the slit facings. Fold the slit facings to the right side and sew across the facings 1" (2.5 cm) above the bottom edge (hemline). Trim the hems on the slit facings.

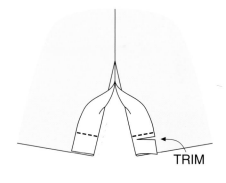

TRIM

Turn the slit facings to the wrong side. Fold the 1" (2.5 cm) hem to the wrong side, press and pin. Sew close to the edge of hem, the edges of slit facings, and across the top edges of facings, as shown. If desired, you can hem the slit facings with a blind hem, see Hems, Page 18.

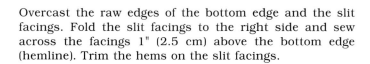

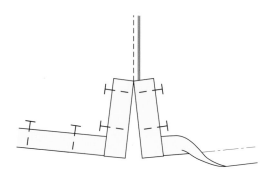

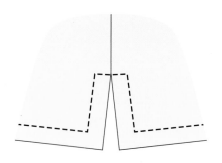

ELASTIC IN CASING

Elastic in a casing can be added to the bottom edge of a pullover top or a T-shirt. You can use 1/4"-3/4" (6 mm-2 cm) wide elastic.

Overcast the bottom edge. To determine the width of the casing, add 1/4" (6 mm) to the width of the elastic you are using. Fold the casing to the wrong side and press. Stitch close to the edge of casing, leaving an opening for inserting the elastic.

Cut one piece of elastic the following length, or measure elastic around the body at the position of the elastic.

XS	S	M	L	XL
31"	34"	37"	40"	43"
(79 cm)	(86 cm)	(94 cm)	(101 cm)	(109 cm)

Insert the elastic into the casing. Overlap the ends of the elastic 3/8" (1 cm) and sew together. Finish sewing the casing seam. Distribute the gathers evenly. To keep the elastic from rolling, sew through all layers across the width of casing at the side seams.

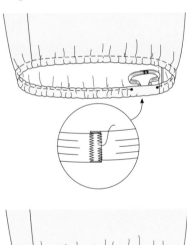

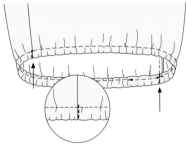

DRAWSTRING

A drawstring can be added to the bottom edge of a pullover top. Use a purchased drawstring, or make a narrow tie from the self fabric. Before hemming the garment, the buttonholes for the drawstring have to be made. Mark the buttonhole placements 1 3/8" (3.5 cm) above the bottom edge and 5/8" (1.5 cm) on each side of the center front.

Pullover top with neckline binding.
Sleeves with cuffs. Elastic in casing.
Straight skirt.
Fabric: Polyester georgette

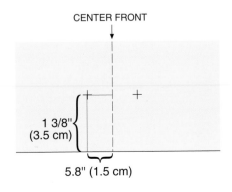

CENTER FRONT

1 3/8"
(3.5 cm)

5.8" (1.5 cm)

74

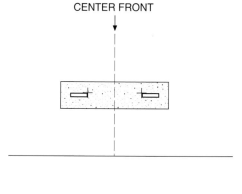

Fuse a small piece of interfacing to the wrong side under the buttonhole placements. Make 3/8" (1 cm) horizontal buttonholes.

Fold 1" (2.5 cm) for the casing to the wrong side and sew close to edge of casing. Insert the drawstring into the casing through the buttonholes.

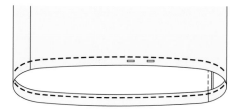

LOOP

A narrow loop from the self fabric, can be used on a neckline with a slit or as a one button closure on an open front jacket or cardigan.

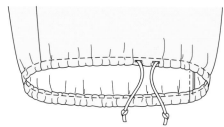

Cut a 3" (7 cm) square piece of fabric on the grain. Fold the square piece diagonally in half, right sides and raw edges together. Sew a scant 1/4" (6 mm) from the folded edge and leave long threads at the end of the seam. Trim the extending fabric 1/8" (3 mm) from the seam.

To turn the loop right side out, thread a large needle with the extending threads. Guide the needle inside the loop to the other end, and pull on the threads to turn.

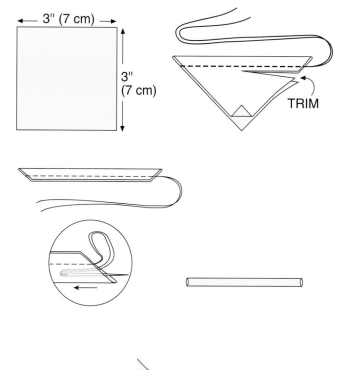

The length of the loop will depend on the size of the button and the seam allowance that is included on the garment. To determine the length, pin one end of the loop to garment and baste along the seam line, pin the other end 1/4" (6 mm) from the first. Check the size of the loop with the button and adjust the length. Stitch across the ends of loop on the seam line and trim the excess length.

NARROW TIES

If making narrow ties from lightweight woven fabric, cut the strip of fabric 1" (2.5 cm) wide on the bias. For cutting bias strips, refer to Page 20.

Fold the strip in half lengthwise, right sides together, and sew the long edge. To turn the tie right side out, use a loop turner or follow these procedures: Cut a small opening on the fold 1/2" (1.3 cm) from one end. Hook a bobby pin through the opening and insert into the tie, guide the bobby pin through the tie to other end, see illustration. Trim the tie at the cut opening.

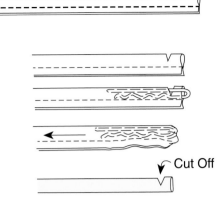

Cut Off

Attach the ties and make knots at the ends.

THREE QUARTER LENGTH SLEEVES

The patterns for the T-shirt and the blouse include short and full length sleeves. If you wish to have three-quarter length sleeves, it is easy to change the pattern.

Trace the sleeve pattern piece; on the blouse, use the line for the sleeve with a hem. Draw a line 4" (10 cm) above the bottom edge of the sleeve. To allow for a smooth hem, add to the sleeve seam as follows: At the bottom of the sleeve pattern, fold up the 1" (2.5 cm) hem and trace the sleeve seam edges, see illustration.

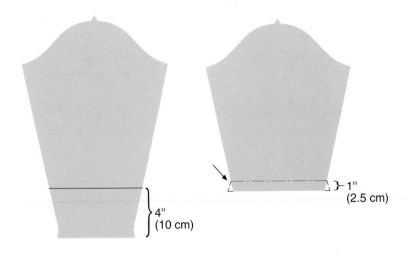

4"
(10 cm)

1"
(2.5 cm)

Pullover top with collar and slit, lengthened 7" (18 cm).
Narrow ties. Side hemline slits.
Three quarter length sleeves. Outline stitching.
Cropped pants.
Fabric: Handkerchief linen

EXTENSIONS

You can add interest to bottom edges of skirts, pants, blouses, and sleeves by making extensions from contrast fabric. Decide on the width of the extension you wish to have and draw a line on the pattern this distance from the bottom edge (be sure to consider the hem allowance). Cut the pattern piece apart on the line and add seam allowances to both the cut edges.

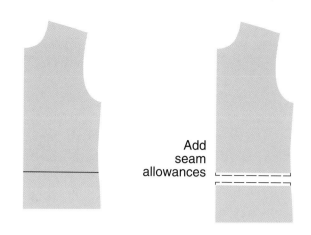

Add
seam
allowances

Sew the extensions to the bottom edges of the pieces and continue to sew as previously described.

PATCHWORK EXTENSIONS

Patchwork extensions add a designer look to your garment. Combine fabrics with different colors and designs, or use fabrics with similar color, but different textures. Make the patterns for the extension as described previously.

Sew scrap pieces of fabric together at random. The following illustrations are shown for procedure only.

Pin two pieces of fabric, right sides together, and sew a straight seam. Press the seam allowances to one side. Trim if necessary, to make one side straight.

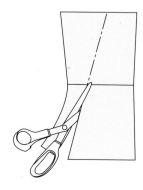

Blouse with scoop neckline and facing. Patchwork extensions.
Basic pants.
Fabric: Rayon velvet

Continue to sew additional pieces, always sewing straight edges together. Trim as necessary, to make the edges straight. Keep sewing pieces together, until the piece is large enough for the extension pattern piece.

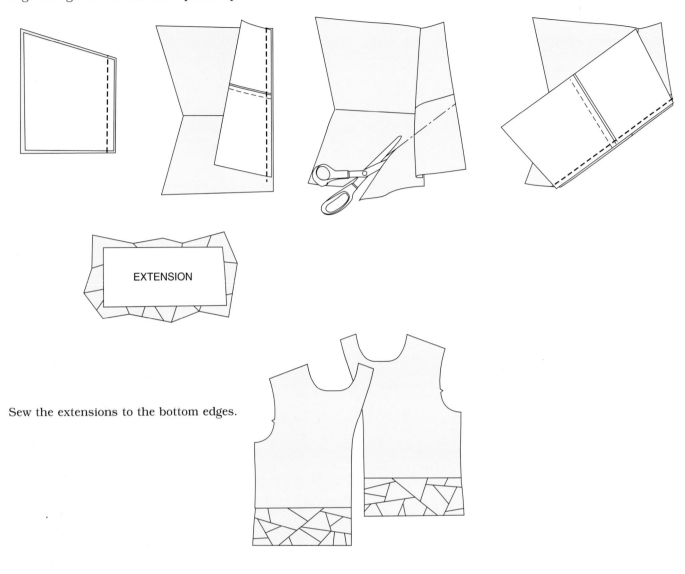

Sew the extensions to the bottom edges.

CONTRAST INSETS

Insets from contrast fabric can make a rather simple design elegant. They can be added to skirts and sleeves, across the width of the garment or lengthwise. Insets can be made from contrast fabrics, such as sheer, chiffon, batiste, voile, georgette, lace or satin. Decide on the position and the width of the inset and draw lines on the pattern the width of the finished inset. Cut the pattern apart on the lines and add seam allowances to all the cut edges. See photo of garment with contrast insets on Page 8.

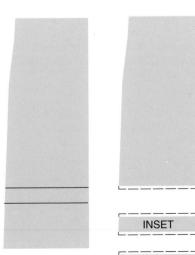

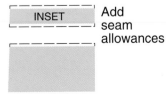

INSET

Add seam allowances

TRIMS

Adding ribbons and trims is an easy way to embellish your garments. Trims can be added to the bottom edges of jackets, sleeves, skirts and pants.

PURCHASED TRIMS

Trims and ribbons vary in width and you can use as many rows as desired. To make an interesting effect, you can combine different trims and ribbons.

When purchasing the trim, be sure to check the recommended care. If you plan to wash the garment, be sure to select a washable trim. In this case, it is a good idea to pre-wash the trim before applying it to the garment; wash by hand and lay flat to dry.

After the garment is completed, pin the trim to the bottom edge of the garment at the position desired. Start at the seam that shows the least, place one end of the trim 1/4" (6 mm) past the seam, pin the trim around the garment, fold under the other end at the seam line, overlapping the ends and pin. Sew on both edges of the trim and across the folded end. When sewing trims and ribbons by machine, it is best to sew both edges in the same direction.

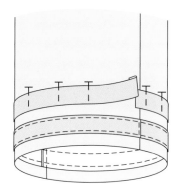

FABRIC TRIMS

You can easily make a trim from any light to medium weight fabric. Cut strips on the crosswise or lengthwise grain, or on the bias. Refer to Page 20 for cutting bias strips. Cut the strips twice the width you wish the finished trim to be.

Fold the edges of the strip to the center and press. Sew the strip to the garment as described for the purchased trim.

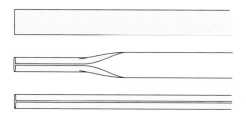

Cropped pants. Trims.
Pullover top with neckline binding.
Fabric: Polyester crepe

APPLIQUES

A fun way to personalize your garment is by adding appliqués. The Master Pattern includes several appliqués that are easy to make. If you wish to have a different size, use a copy machine to enlarge or reduce the size. You can combine the designs or use them individually. Basic instructions for applying appliqués are included. For more information, alternate methods, and a great variety of appliqués, see the book *Appliqué the Kwik Sew Way*, by Kerstin Martensson.

USING PAPER BACKED FUSIBLE WEB

For this type of appliqué, you will need fabric pieces for the appliqué, paper backed fusible web and "tear-away material".

Select the appliqué design and the fabric. For soft or lightweight fabrics, stabilize the fabric pieces with a lightweight fusible interfacing, this will make it easier to sew, especially if you are using a knit fabric or a fabric that ravels.

Trace the design to the paper side of the fusible web. **Note**: The finished appliqué will be the mirror image of the original. Place the web side to the wrong side of the appliqué fabric and fuse.

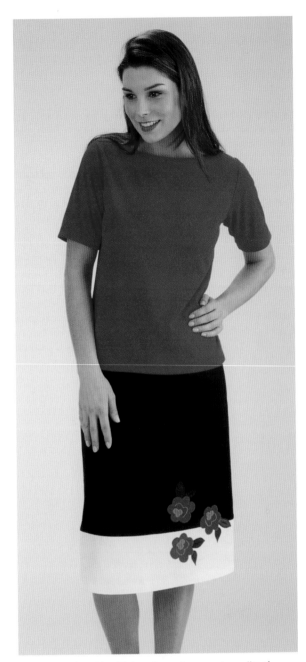

Straight skirt. Extensions. Layered appliqué.
Top with boat neckline.
Fabric: Skirt - rayon faille. Top - cotton interlock

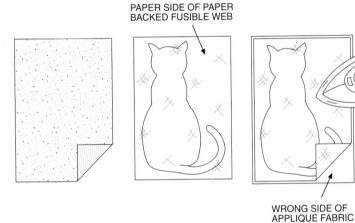

PAPER SIDE OF PAPER
BACKED FUSIBLE WEB

WRONG SIDE OF
APPLIQUE FABRIC

Cut out the appliqué and remove the paper backing. Place the appliqué to the garment at the desired position and fuse in place. Place a piece of "tear-away material" on the wrong side of the garment under the appliqué and pin or baste in place. The "tear-away material" prevents puckering and stretching while satin stitching. Satin stitch over all the raw edges.

PAPER
BACKING

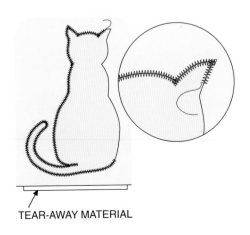

TEAR-AWAY MATERIAL

80

SATIN STITCHING

Set the zigzag to a slightly wider than medium width and a very short stitch length 35 to 50 stitches per inch (15 to 20 stitches per centimeter). Loosen the top thread tension so that the top thread is pulled to the underside and the bobbin thread does not show on the right side. Try the stitches on a scrap piece of the same fabric you are using, adjust the stitches so the appliqué fabric does not show through and the stitches are not piled up.

Outside corners: On the outside corner, lower the needle into the background fabric, pivot, and continue satin stitching.

Inside corners: On the inside corner, lower the needle into the appliqué, pivot, and continue satin stitching.

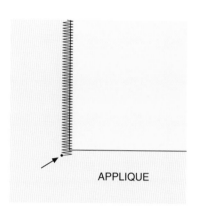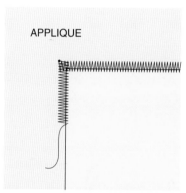

Curves: To make smooth curves, stop at close intervals with the needle in the fabric, raise the presser foot, and turn the appliqué slightly. For the inside curves, lower the needle inside the appliqué, for the outside curves, lower the needle on the background fabric.

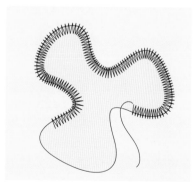

Points: To make a point, gradually reduce the width of the stitches. When you reach the point, pivot and satin stitch the other side, gradually increasing the width of the stitches.

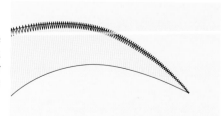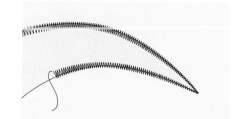

LAYERED APPLIQUE

A layered appliqué design requires more than one fabric. We will use a flower design as an example. Note: The finished design will be the mirror image of the original. Select the fabrics for the flower, leaves and the center of the flower. Trace the design to the paper side of paper backed fusible web, tracing each part that will be from different fabrics separately. When tracing the leaves, extend leaves slightly, to be able to place the leaves under the flower, see illustration.

PAPER SIDE OF PAPER BACKED FUSIBLE WEB

Place the web side of the paper backed fusible web to the wrong side of the appliqué fabric for each part and fuse.

PAPER-BACKED FUSIBLE WEB

WRONG SIDE OF APPLIQUE FABRIC

Cut out the appliqué pieces. Remove the paper backing and fuse the pieces to the garment in the following order: Leaves, flower and center of flower. Transfer the detail lines to the leaves and the flower.

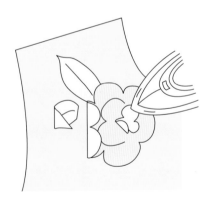

Place a piece of "tear-away material" on the wrong side under the appliqué and pin or baste in place. Satin stitch the appliqué to the garment and satin stitch the detail lines. Remove the "tear-away material."

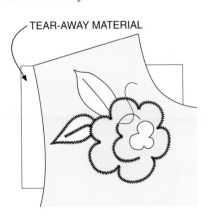

TEAR-AWAY MATERIAL

APPLIQUES FROM PRINT FABRIC

An easy way to make an appliqué is to purchase a piece of fabric with a design you like, it can be a flower, or any other design. Be sure to purchase enough fabric to get the complete design. Or, if you have a design on the fabric you are using for a skirt, pants or shorts, you may want to cut out part of the design and use it as an appliqué on a blouse or top for a coordinated outfit.

Cut around the design, allowing extra fabric all the way around. If the fabric is lightweight or stretchy, stabilize the fabric on the wrong side with lightweight fusible interfacing. Use paper backed fusible web and fuse to the wrong side of the design. Cut out the design.

Remove the paper backing and fuse the appliqué to the garment. Satin stitch as described previously.

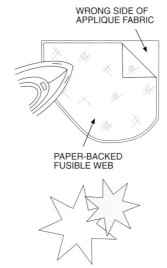

WRONG SIDE OF APPLIQUE FABRIC

PAPER-BACKED FUSIBLE WEB

OUTLINE STITCHING

Any of the appliqué designs can be done with outline stitching. Outline stitching is satin stitching which forms the design. Note: The finished design will be the mirror image of the original.

Cut a piece of "tear-away material" a few inches larger than the appliqué design. Trace the design to the "tear-away material". Mark the placement of the design on the right side of the garment. Place the "tear-away material" with the traced lines on the **wrong side** of the garment at the position of design and pin or baste in place. Transfer the design to the right side of the garment by sewing over the traced lines, using a straight stitch. Use a slightly contrast color thread on the bobbin so the lines can easily be seen on the right side of the garment.

On the right side, satin stitch over the straight stitches. Remove the "tear-away material" on the wrong side.

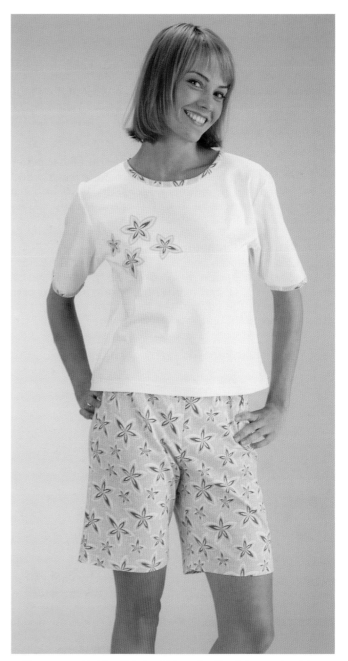

Sleepwear, T-shirt. Fabric edging. Appliqué from print fabric. Shorts.
Fabric: Cotton Interlock

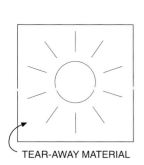

TEAR-AWAY MATERIAL

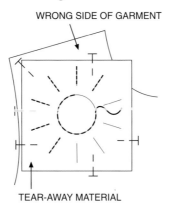

WRONG SIDE OF GARMENT

TEAR-AWAY MATERIAL

SLEEPWEAR

Nightshirts and pajamas can easily be made, using the T-shirt or the blouse patterns. For pajama bottoms, use the pants or shorts pattern. If you wish to use knit fabric, use the T-shirt pattern, for woven fabrics, use the blouse pattern. You may want to make the garment one size larger than you otherwise use, for a more comfortable fit.

To make a nightshirt, using the T-shirt or the blouse pattern, for a finished length of 26" (66 cm) from the waist, add 20 1/2" (52 cm) to the bottom edge of the front and back pattern pieces. Add 30 1/2" (77 cm) for a 36" (91 cm) finished length from the waist.

EASY NECKLINE FINISHES
If making a pullover from knit fabric, the neckline can be finished with a narrow hem. Overcast the neckline edge and fold a 3/8" (1 cm) hem to the wrong side and press. Stitch close to the edge of the hem with a narrow zigzag stitch or topstitch, using a double needle.

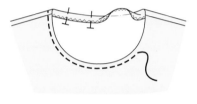

Another easy way to finish the neckline is by using stretch lace. Use stretch lace 3/8"- 5/8" (1 cm -1.5 cm) wide.

Sew one shoulder seam. Place the stretch lace to the neckline with right sides up and the edge of lace even with the neckline edge. Stitch close to the inner edge of the lace, using a medium zigzag width and a slightly shorter than medium stitch length.

Trim the fabric under the stretch lace close to the stitches. Sew the other shoulder seam.

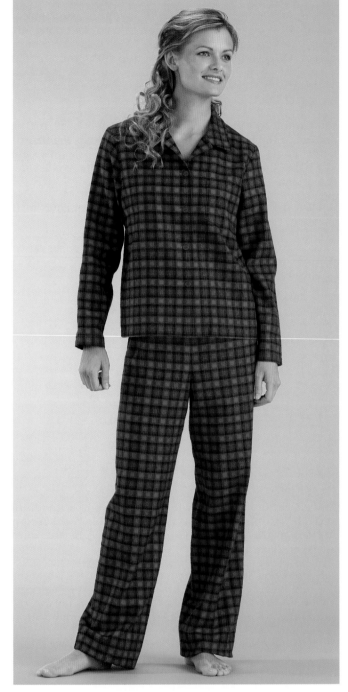

Sleepwear, Basic Blouse. Hemmed sleeves. Breast pocket.
Pants. Drawstring waist.
Fabric: Cotton flannel

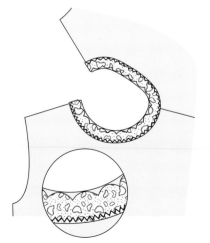

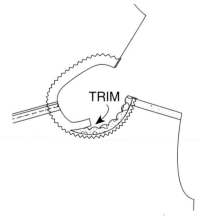

TRIM

KWIK•SEW has over 800 patterns in the pattern line and include patterns for misses, women's plus sizes, men, children, toddlers, babies, crafts and accessories The instructions and illustrations are very clear and easy to follow. The patterns are printed on white heavy paper, not flimsy tissue paper, so when you have to reposition the pattern pieces on the fabric, it will not tear and the pattern can be used over and over again.

KWIK SERGE patterns are especially designed so at least one view can be made completely on the serger (overlock) machine. The designs are very easy to make, whether you make them on the serger (overlock) or a regular sewing machine. Instructions are included for both the serger (overlock) machine and the standard sewing machine. Look for patterns that have the logo: KWIK Serge.

KWIK START Learn-to-sew patterns are especially designed for beginner sewers and anyone who wants to learn to sew. These patterns are very simple and include special easy-to-follow sewing instructions with many more illustrations.

All KWIK•SEW patterns include four or five sizes in each pattern envelope. Like the Master Pattern included with this book, each size is printed in a different color to make it easy to cut out or trace your size. KWIK•SEW patterns are printed on one side of the paper, you can cut out the size you want or trace the pattern, if you wish to use the other sizes.

Most patterns are sized XS-S-M-L-XL. All patterns are designed to fit specific body measurements with basic and design ease. Basic ease is added to make the garment comfortable to wear, design ease varies with the fashion and the style of the garment.

Seam allowances are included on all the patterns. Some patterns have 1/4" (6 mm) seam allowances and others have 5/8" (1.5 cm). The seam allowances are given on each pattern piece. Be sure to always read the instruction sheet before you start to sew.

Select a pattern with a design that fits your sewing ability, usually the more pieces and details in a design, the more difficult it is to make the garment. A complicated design can leave you frustrated, while a simple design will be easy and fun to sew.

It is best to select the pattern first and then purchase the fabric and the notions for your project. It is very important to read the back of the pattern envelope for the recommended fabrics and the description, which describes the garment and the details that cannot easily be seen.

If the pattern is designed for stretch knits, the back of the envelope has a stretch chart. You should test the fabric for the correct amount of stretch. Patterns designed for stretch knits have less ease than patterns designed for woven fabrics, the greater the amount of stretch, the smaller the pattern pieces will be. For example, patterns for swimsuits are smaller than the body measurements and require fabrics with 75% stretch.

KWIK•SEW has all the great styles you are looking for. Try a KWIK•SEW pattern and see how easy and fun sewing can be. You can find KWIK•SEW patterns in most fabric stores.

To see the complete line of KWIK•SEW patterns and books, visit **www.kwiksew.com.**

The fabric requirements are given for the basic garments only. If using variations or changing the lengths, use the fabric and notion requirements only as a guide.

Fabric requirement allows for nap, one way design or shading. Extra fabric may be needed to match the design or for shrinkage.

T-SHIRT

(ALL NECKLINES, EXCEPT SHIRT WITH HOOD AND COWL COLLAR)
Suggested fabrics - Stretch knits only with 25% stretch across the grain such as: Interlock, jersey, textured knits, stretch velour, pointelle jersey, thermal knits

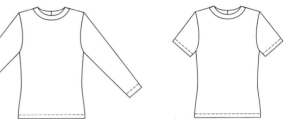

The finished length at the center back from the natural neckline

XS	S	M	L	XL
20 3/4"	21"	21 1/2"	22"	22 1/4"
52.5 cm	53.5 cm	55 cm	56 cm	56 cm

Fabric 60" (152 cm) wide
LONG SLEEVES
  All Sizes 1 5/8 yd (1.50 m)
SHORT SLEEVES
  All Sizes 1 1/4 yd (1.15 m)
Optional Ribbing 28" (70 cm) wide
Crew Neckband 4" (10 cm) - All sizes
Mock Turtleneck 6" (15 cm) - All sizes
Notions: Thread.

SHIRT WITH HOOD OR COWL COLLAR
Additional 1/4 yd (0.25 m) fabric required.

BASIC BLOUSE & BLOUSE WITH SCOOP NECKLINE AND FACING

Suggested fabrics - Light to medium weight woven fabrics such as: Broadcloth, chambray, sheeting, lightweight denim, rayon and blends, challis, silk types, crepe

The finished length at the center back from the natural neckline

XS	S	M	L	XL
20 3/4"	21"	21 1/2"	22"	22 1/4"
52.5 cm	53.5 cm	55 cm	56 cm	56.5 cm

Fabric 45" (115 cm) wide
LONG SLEEVES with or without cuff
  All sizes 2 1/8 yd (1.95 m)
SHORT SLEEVES
  All sizes 1 7/8 yd (1.75 m)
Fabric 60" (152 cm) wide
LONG SLEEVES with or without cuff
  Sizes XS-S 1 1/2 yd (1.40 m)
  Sizes M-L-XL 1 3/4 yd (1.60 m)
SHORT SLEEVES
  Sizes XS-S-M 1 3/8 yd (1.30 m)
  Size L 1 1/2 yd (1.40 m)
  Size XL 1 3/4 yd (1.60 m)

Notions: Thread, lightweight fusible interfacing.
Basic blouse: 5/8" (15 mm) buttons - four for short sleeves; six for sleeves with cuffs. Blouse with scoop neckline and facing: 5/8" (15 mm) buttons - five for short sleeves; seven for sleeves with cuffs.

PANTS, CROPPED PANTS & SHORTS

Suggested fabrics - Light to medium weight woven and firm knit fabrics such as: Cotton, cotton types, challis, crepe, rayon and blends, twill, French terry, flannel, double knit, jersey

PANTS

Finished inside leg seam 30" (76 cm) All sizes
Fabric 45" (115 cm) wide
  Sizes XS-S 2 1/2 yd (2.30 m)
  Size M 2 5/8 yd (2.40 m)
  Sizes L-XL 2 3/4 yd (2.55 m)
Fabric 60" (152 cm) wide
  Sizes XS-S-M 1 5/8 yd (1.50 m)
  Sizes L-XL 2 1/4 yd (2.10 m)
Notions: Thread, 1 yd (0.95 m) of 1" (2.5 cm) wide elastic.

CROPPED PANTS

Finished inside leg seam 25" (63 cm) All sizes
Fabric 45" (115 cm) wide
  Size XS 2 1/4 yd (2.10 m)
  Sizes S-M-L 2 3/8 yd (2.20 m)
  Size XL 2 1/2 yd (2.30 m)
Fabric 60" (152 cm) wide
  Sizes XS-S-M 1 1/2 yd (1.40 m)
  Sizes L-XL 2 yd (1.85 m)
Notions: Thread, 1 yd (0.95 m) of 1" (2.5 cm) wide elastic.

SHORTS

Finished inside leg seam 9" (23 cm) All sizes
Fabric 45" (115 cm) wide
  Size XS 1 3/8 yd (1.30 m)
  Sizes S-M-L 1 1/2 yd (1.40 m)
  Size XL 1 5/8 yd (1.50 m)
Fabric 60" (152 cm) wide
  Size XS 1 yd (0.95 m)
  Sizes S-M-L-XL 1 1/8 yd (1.05 m)
Notions: Thread, 1 yd (0.95 m) of 1" (2.5 cm) wide elastic.

SKIRTS

Suggested fabrics - Light to medium weight woven and firm knit fabrics such as: Cotton types, linen, lightweight soft denim, rayon and blends, crepe, challis, silk types, jersey, matte jersey, double knits

Finished length 26" (66 cm) All sizes.

STRAIGHT SKIRT

Fabric 45" (115 cm) wide
  Sizes XS-S 7/8 yd (0.80 m)
  Sizes M-L-XL 1 3/4 yd (1.60 m)
Fabric 60" (152 cm) wide
  All Sizes 7/8 yd (0.80 m)
Notions: 1 yd (0.95 m) of 1" (2.5 cm) wide elastic

GORED SKIRT

Fabric 45" (115 cm) wide
  All Sizes 1 3/4 yd (1.60 m)
Fabric 60" (152 cm) wide
  All Sizes 1 3/4 yd (1.60 m)
Notions: Thread, 1 yd (0.95 m) of 1" (2.5 cm) wide elastic.

ABOUT THE AUTHOR

Easy Sewing the KWIK•SEW Way is the latest addition to a series of books on home sewing by Kerstin Martensson. Her previous best selling books have achieved world-wide success and popularity. The overwhelming acceptance of Kerstin Martensson's books can be attributed to the illustrated, easy-to-follow, step-by-step procedures. Over two million copies of her books have been sold thus far. Many of these are being used by schools and colleges as sewing textbooks.

Kerstin Martensson is the President of KWIK•SEW Pattern Company, Inc., and is internationally known for her innovative approach to sewing. Kerstin was born in Gothenburg, Sweden and educated in both Sweden and England. She specialized in clothing construction, pattern design, and fashion.

Kerstin has traveled extensively throughout the United States, Canada, Australia, England, and the Scandinavian countries, lecturing on her techniques to make sewing faster, easier, and more fun.

Kerstin founded KWIK•SEW Pattern Company, Inc. in 1967 to make patterns for stretch fabric, as at the time none of the established pattern companies had patterns for this type of fabric. The company has grown into a world-wide operation with subsidiaries in Australia, Canada and New Zealand, plus distributors in Europe. There are over eight hundred pattern in the KWIK•SEW pattern line and now includes patterns for all types of fabric.

Kerstin is encouraged by her customers' overwhelming response to her patterns and books, and she is dedicated to bring the most up-to-date fashion and sewing techniques to the home sewer.

This book was written with the help of all the skilled staff in the Design and Art Departments of KWIK•SEW Pattern Company. Their combined talents have resulted in a book that is full of creative ideas and illustrations. Discover how much fun it is to sew.